1

We Begin with a Simple Thesis . . .

Copy 1

1

*S*ociety is undergoing a fundamental transformation from the Industrial Age to the Information Age. This is a global phenomenon with very significant local implications. All people, organizations, societies, and nations are affected, although not at the same pace or to the same degree. Those who realign their practices most effectively to Information Age standards will reap substantial benefits. Those who do not will be replaced or diminished by more nimble competitors.

Realignment to the Needs of the Information Age

Realignment to the needs of the Information Age requires more than increasing the use of information technology. Many organizations have merely superimposed a silicon veneer onto outmoded Industrial Age systems, techniques, and organizational cultures. Then they puzzle why gains in productivity and competitiveness prove elusive.

Realignment to the imperatives of the Information Age begins with an assessment of how the needs of one's stakeholders, clients, customers, and beneficiaries will change in the Information Age. Guided by this understanding, organizations can determine how they must change their structures, roles, and functions to serve those needs. Every organization we studied that has developed such a vision for the Information Age has realized the necessity for fundamental change and realignment.

Higher education has invested—often painfully—in information technology infrastructure and in restructuring our organizations, redefining roles and responsibilities of employees, and re-engineering our systems and processes. While we have changed a great deal, American higher education has not transformed. The reasons are clear. We have not yet formulated a compelling vision for the learning required to succeed in the Information Age. Absent this vision, we have not reshaped structures, roles, functions, and services to address those changing needs.

We are moving from our existing, Industrial Age model for education to a learning vision for the 21st century—a vision that is fundamentally realigned with the needs of learners in the Information Age. The pathway from the existing world, where colleges and universities substantially "own" the teaching franchise, leads to a world where the learning franchise is spread among many providers and new types of facilitators, learning agents, and intermediaries. This new world holds greater competition and more choices—and substantial opportunities to serve legions of Information Age learners.

In the Industrial Age, the capabilities of new technologies improve the efficiency of existing academic processes. Such applications have not been designed to impact on academic productivity. In the Information Age, the power of the learning vision will pull forward new uses of information technology that will facilitate and enable the transitions to the Information Age. These applications will greatly enhance the productivity of learning systems to meet rapidly expanding demand for learning opportunities.

Transformation-guided planning requires "looking around the curvature of the earth" to foresee futures that we cannot foretell with precision. Institutions need not begin a revolution, but rather adjust existing processes and initiatives toward transformative ends.

This monograph will help you establish a vision framework for transformation. It is meant to be provocative, not definitive. It is neither a comprehensive review of research and the literature nor an attempt to "prove" our assertions about the possibilities awaiting learning intermediaries who can meet the needs of Information Age learners. Now is the time to think strategically and position

institutions to consider pathways to transformation and act on them, not to engage in preemptive debate. This does not mean we lack evidence to support our assessments of current conditions and future opportunities. Precisely the opposite is true. But our experience with envisioning and developing Information Age tools suggests that if we wait until the vision is perfectly clear and risks have vanished, the opportunities will have passed, as well.

Industrial Age	Information Age
Teaching franchise	Learning franchise
Provider-driven, set time for learning	Individualized learning
Information infrastructure as support tool	Information infrastructure as the fundamental instrument of transformation
Individual technologies	Technology synergies
Time out for education	Just-in-time learning
Continuing education	Perpetual learning
Separate learning systems	Fused learning systems
Traditional courses, degrees, and academic calendars	Unbundled learning experiences based on learner needs
Teaching and certification of mastery are combined	Learning and certification of mastery are related, yet separable issues
Front-end, lump-sum payment based on length of academic process	Point-of-access payment for exchange of intellectual property based on value added
Collections of fragmented, narrow, and proprietary systems	Seamless, integrated, comprehensive, and open systems
Bureaucratic systems	Self-informing, self-correcting systems
Rigid, predesigned processes	Families of transactions customizable to the needs of learners, faculty, and staff
Technology push	Learning vision pull

2

Paradigm Lost, Paradigm Found

- **All the World Is Before Us**

- **The Information Age Will Be Learner-Driven**

- **To the Brink of Transformation**

*T*he Information Age is being driven by learning and knowledge. The rate of knowledge generation and the corresponding demand for its use are exponentially larger than in the Industrial Age. The life cycle of information will continually shrink. Demand for effective learning opportunities will also increase dramatically. By our reckoning, the 1990s mark the first decade of the Information Age. These early transition stages of the Information Age present extraordinary opportunities to higher education. So the time is right to develop a compelling vision for learning in the 21st century.

All the World Is Before Us

The Information Age is an epoch where "higher education" could occupy *the* pivotal role in society. It is a time when demand for learning is anticipated to skyrocket, but resources available under existing models for educational delivery are expected to remain fairly static. Fresh vision is needed to create new delivery systems for learning, new paradigms for financing, and new models for higher education.

Without continued innovation, we may be doomed to fail. Our existing models are in many cases inadequate to the challenge. Currently, there are 3,613 institutions of higher education in the United States. Together they enroll 15.1 million students—equivalent to approximately 12 million full-time enrollments—and spend $156 billion per year in operations. They serve a mixture of traditional students and some learners from the workforce. Yet, as the Information Age develops, substantially greater numbers of workers will require types of learning opportunities not currently available. The potential magnitude of this demand may be overwhelming.

Looking to the year 2000, futurists estimate that just to keep even each individual in the workforce will need to accumulate learning equivalent to that currently associated with 30 credit hours of instruction, every seven years. This level of learning will be needed for every member of the Information Age workforce who wishes to remain competitive and productive—perhaps even to maintain basic employment. This can translate into the full-time equivalent (FTE) enrollment of one-seventh of the workforce, at any point in time. Since there will be an estimated 141 million workers in the U.S. in the year 2000, this could equal over 20 million FTE learners from the workforce. Most will be new learners. Using our existing educational model, these learners would require an additional 672 campuses with an enrollment of 30,000 students each. At an estimate of $350 million each, the 672 campuses would cost $235 billion to build and an additional $217 billion per year to operate. To meet the full potential demand by the year 2010, a campus would have to be opened every eight days. Even if this demand were served by a mixture of higher education and other learning intermediaries, the cost under existing approaches to educational finance would be exorbitant.

This is not merely an issue for American higher education. The table on the next page details the size of the labor force and extrapolates the number of FTE Information Age learners from the workforce in the U.S. and nine other industrialized countries. It then projects the number of campuses under this scenario required to serve them, and the

Information
Age

Industrial
Age

Estimated Labor Force and Annualized New FTE Learners by A.D. 2000

Country	Labor Force 2000	FTE Learners	Campuses	Cost to Build Campuses
United States	141.1M	20.2M	672	$235.2B
Japan	64.3M	9.2M	306	$107.2B
Germany	37.2M	5.3M	177	$ 62.0B
United Kingdom	29.1M	4.2M	139	$ 48.5B
France	25.8M	3.7M	123	$ 43.0B
Italy	24.2M	3.5M	115	$ 40.3B
Spain	15.7M	2.2M	75	$ 26.2B
Canada	14.6M	2.1M	70	$ 24.3B
Australia	8.9M	1.3M	42	$ 14.8B
Sweden	4.6M	.7M	22	$ 7.7B
World	2,752.5M	100.0M+	3,300	—

Sources: 1) *Johnston, William B., "Global Work Force 2000: The New World Labor Market,"* Harvard Business Review, *March/ April 1991. 2) Estimates of FTE Learners developed at Invited Futurist Conference, Claremont, California, October 1994. 3) Estimates of Number of Campuses and Costs driven by average statistics, California State University, 1992.*

cost to build the new campuses. A world total is also estimated. Even if one assumes that the ratio of knowledge workers in countries other than these nine is much smaller—say only one in four— this still yields a total potential learning pool of over 100 million FTE learners.

These estimates of learner demand may seem too high. Nevertheless, they are a good starting point for discussion. Whether the number of net new learners is five million or 25 million is immaterial. Whatever the level, this represents a major new opportunity. These projections cannot be validated in the absence of two movements that will require fully five to 10 years or more to develop. First, society must complete its transition to an Information Age economic model to create the full measure of demand. Second, learning opportunities must embrace the needs of Information Age learners. In the absence of genuine Information Age options, the latent demand will not materialize as actual learners.

On the other hand, the figures may be too conservative. Some futurists suggest that many Information Age workers will need to spend at least 20 percent of their time engaged in learning. Every day. This would translate into as many as 28 million FTE learners in the U.S. workforce alone. And in a networked learning environment, knowledge knows no borders of geography or time. So, the most facile learning mechanisms will serve an international market of knowledge workers. The software engineer in Bombay, the venture capitalist in Frankfurt, the corporate accountant in London, the biotechnologist in Hong Kong, and the flexible manufacturing technician in Beijing are all in this marketplace. Many of these learners are seeking both subject area competence and English language instruction—the international language of business and science. However one looks at the learning needs for the Information Age, the demand is huge. And the reason is simple. There are powerful societal forces at work driving the transformation of education. And these forces are inexorable.

The Information Age Will Be Learner-Driven

The teaching franchise will be joined by an emerging learning franchise. Both will be important in the Information Age.

What do we mean by the "teaching franchise"? It is the current system by which teaching and the awarding of course credits and degrees are bundled together seamlessly in accredited institutions of higher education. The awarding of course and degree credit is warranted by credentialed faculty. Exclusive rights to the teaching franchise are granted by regional accrediting associations. These associations are empowered by the collective of institutions and the Federal government, which restricts Federal financial aid to appropriately accredited institutions. In many states, coordinating agencies also warrant the franchise.

On the other hand, the learning franchise provides access to powerful learning systems, information and knowledge bases, scholarly exchange net-

Learning Franchise

Teaching Franchise

Existing and Potential FTE Learners	
Existing Learners—Industrial Age, U.S.	12M
New Learners—Information Age, U.S.	20–28M
New Learners—Information Age, Global	100M+

Nobody "Owns" the Learning Franchise

- **Network learning eliminates barriers to entry.**

- **New roles will emerge—facilitators, intermediaries, learning agents.**

- **Higher education needs to embrace transformation to compete for the learning franchise.**

Higher education has already passed one significant milestone on its way to the Information Age: more older students are enrolled in higher education than are 18–22 year-olds—the traditional undergraduate students. Many institutions are grappling with the challenge of understanding and serving these learners' needs. But neither these learners nor our institutions fully understand the implications of perpetual learning as a style in the Information Age.

Electronic classrooms, information networks to augment classroom instruction, distance learning, continuing education, and contract learning are examples of higher education's commitment to extended education. Interactive, multi-media systems are growing in use. Some institutions are offering on-line learning—University of Phoenix, On-Line University, Magellan University, National Technological University, and the Virtual University, for example. However, these are only transitional efforts, not transformational. The basic metaphors for instruction have remained fundamentally unchanged in most settings. Technology has been used to improve their efficiency, not transform them. If higher education is to play the major role in the learning franchise for the Information Age, a genuinely transformative vision is a necessity.

works, or other mechanisms for the delivery of learning. Learning modules and systems are open to anyone who wishes to access them and has the resources to compensate the provider. Measurement and certification of mastery will be important for many learners, but they will be separable from the learning franchise.

The race is on to determine ownership of the learning franchise for the Information Age. Network learning eliminates many of the barriers to entry currently present in the Learning Industry. It provides opportunities for many new facilitators, intermediaries, and learning agents. An array of organizations is positioned to vie for new opportunities—institutions of higher education, corporations, technology companies, for-profit education enterprises, and research laboratories. New strategic alliances and commercial ventures will be formed to tap these potentials.

To the Brink of Transformation

Higher education is at a crossroads. Having aligned its operations and output with the needs of the Industrial Age, it has settled into a mode of operation that is often likened to the "factory" of the age it served. The "factory model" has served the Industrial Age well. It focuses on the classic factors of production—inputs, processes, outputs. This model is insufficiently flexible to accommodate the rapid changes of the Information Age. It relies on certification of the quality of inputs and the quality of the process, rather than on measurement of outcomes. The factory model is very costly. The costs associated with providing the required level of educational opportunity to an additional 20 million FTE learners also suggests that the factory model will not meet the demands of the Information Age—from either a service or a cost perspective.

The use of the term "factory model" conjures up visions of a Dickensian world of smokestacks and ink ledgers. Surely such an allusion is inappropriate to American colleges and universities, whose campuses are thoroughly modern and awash in technology. In reality the basic patterns and cadences of academic life predate even the Industrial Revolution. But the processes and organizations perfected during the maturation of the renowned American higher education system during the 1960s–1980s are classic, late Industrial Age design. Referring to these as a "factory model" in an intentionally hyperbolic manner dramatizes the contradiction of laying Information Age tools atop a basic system of values, functions, and structures that remain unchanged.

Transformation operates in an inescapable context of fiscal stringency. In fact, until now, fiscal crisis rather than transformational intent has dominated the focus of change efforts in American higher education over the past decade. Institutions have responded to the onset of severe fiscal restraint through an evolving series of reactions. A typical cycle includes retrenchment, reorganization, and restructuring. Many institutions have added

The Industrial Age (Factory Model) is Characterized by:

- insufficient flexibility;
- focusing on processes and outputs, not outcomes; and
- high cost.

a fourth "R"—"reallocation" to capture resources and reallocate them to programs and initiatives of higher priority. However, even reallocation that is conducted without a vision of new learner needs falls short of its promise.

Taken as a whole, retrenchment, reorganization, restructuring, and reallocation activities have helped institutions develop capabilities and skills that can enable transformation. But they are not

> Remember: Just because we are changing a great deal does not mean we are transforming.

in themselves transformative. They have not addressed the fundamental environmental shifts in learning needs for the Information Age. And they can lead educators to believe, mistakenly, that they have transformed their institutions—or are well on the way to doing so. In reality, even the educators and institutions that have been most aggressive in responding to the environmental challenges of the 1990s have only moved their institutions to the brink of transformation.

Three simple questions must be answered by political leaders, educational leaders, faculty, students, and other stakeholders contemplating the future of higher education. First, "Is today's Industrial Age educational model appropriate to the learning needs of the Information Age—for either traditional learners or learners in the workplace?" Second, "Is society willing to pay for a 20th century 'Industrial Age' model in the 21st century 'Information Age'?" And third, "Can academe afford to miss the opportunity of reshaping itself to serve the emerging needs of the Information Age learner?" If the answers to these questions are no, then genuine transformation is the only acceptable metaphor for bringing postsecondary education into alignment with the emerging needs of learners and society in the Information Age. ◯

3

What Is Transformation?

- Learning Vignettes from the Information Age

- The Four Components of Transformation

*T*ransformation is for everyone, but it is not an all-or-nothing proposition. The classroom will not disappear, nor will the campus fade into oblivion. Rather, American higher education in the 21st century will provide a spectrum of choices for learners, ranging from the truly traditional to the totally transformed. These choices will be exercised by individual learners, faculty, researchers, and practitioners in their daily work and as they chart the pathways for their learning careers.

Individual learners are an inexorable force driving learning in the Information Age. But organizational actions and strategies can either facilitate or limit the choices available to learners. The following illustrative learning vignettes from the Information Age are drawn from the not-too-distant future. They illustrate the power of learner choice.

K athleen, a middle manager of a Denver-based Fortune 500 firm, is called to her Vice President's office for a one-on-one conference. Beginning next year, her job will be eliminated as part of a restructuring of operations. She will be given top priority for a new opening six months from now, but it will require some new skills—a working knowledge of computer networks, an understanding of automated accounting systems, and some familiarity with decision support systems. Encouraged by the preferential opportunity, but challenged by her lack of necessary skills, she uses her office network to contact the local university for access to the required subject expertise.

The university's "smart" application process asks her to convey her needs. After completing this process, she is invited to begin her studies immediately. Upon answering "yes," she is handed over to the instructional management system. The system automatically adds her name and e-mail account to the rosters for the learning spaces for computer networking, automated accounting systems, and decision support systems. Her application, academic records, and specific interests and competency requirements are forwarded instantly to the faculty coordinator of each learning space.

A faculty member for computer networks automatically sends Kathleen the following on-line materials: syllabus, textual materials, and tutorials. As Kathleen proceeds through the introductory tutorial, an expert system monitors her progress and prepares the next learning module, informing the faculty mentor of her progress. A plan for on-line and/or personal conferences, group work sessions, seminars, and other meeting opportunities is negotiated between Kathleen and her mentor.

Learning Vignette #1
Facilitating Employment Transitions

The automated accounting systems faculty member organizes the learning space differently. Each new learner automatically receives a knowledge base evaluation test to assess the learner's existing understanding of the principles of accounting and automated systems. Comparing Kathleen's evaluation to her specified needs and competency requirements, the faculty member constructs a learning program designed specifically for her.

The faculty member for the decision support systems learning space immediately prescribes a decision simulator linked to a theory engine to drive the simulator. As Kathleen works through simulated decisions, the theory engine automatically presents the explanations of the theory behind each element.

Kathleen successfully completes the required level of mastery in four months and gets the job.

Stephanie is just finishing her fresh-man year at a distinguished liberal arts college in Minnesota. She selected this college because of its reputation for excellence and the opportunity to engage with faculty members in small classes. The college has proven to be everything she expected—and more.

Learning Vignette #2

Liberal Arts Colleges Prepare Perpetual Learners

The initial meetings of her small classes set the tone. Most of the faculty do not require traditional textbooks. Some use print-on-demand selections of readings and notes developed by the faculty. Most faculty place required read-ings, faculty notes, and textual materials on the campus network, to be accessed by the student and read before class. Classroom sessions focus on applications, interpretations of concepts, and discus-sion of other perspectives which students discover in their own readings.

All classes require considerable writ-ing and research. Stephanie uses the text and graphics capabilities available through word processing packages, although she draws the material from a rich array of sources—books, CD–ROM discs, videos, and on-line resources. Over time, she be-gins to experiment with hypertext, more

advanced computer graphics, and even simulation. Her final research paper during her freshman term is developed in collaboration with a five-person team and fulfills requirements for three of her courses.

She is also involved in a student-facilitated interest group on environ-mental issues, particularly environmental impact studies. Through this group, she develops a close working relationship with Carol, a student about to graduate, whom Stephanie considers a role model. She plans to follow Carol's example and accelerate her program of study to posi-tion herself for learning and employment after graduation.

Carol demonstrated her mastery of basic critical thinking skills in three years. She began a summer internship with a major accounting firm after her sophomore year, even though she was not a business major. Her fourth year was an exciting combination of directed study and research in collaboration with mentors on the faculty and at the accounting firm. After her upcoming graduation, she plans to join the accounting firm and attend a six-week, full-immersion course to enable her to take the CPA exam. Carol and her employer have already identified a three-year plan of just-in-time learning to guide her initial project experiences and enable her to demonstrate mastery in corporate financial management.

Professor Reynolds directs the graduate programs in higher education administration at a major metropolitan university. He has just completed an evaluation of his accomplishments and is planning his personal learning and work agenda for the coming year. For the past seven years he facilitated the creation of a new approach to graduate learning.

Learners enter the program as a gateway to perpetual collaboration with faculty, researchers, and problem solvers in the field. Many of the learners received their basic education before the widespread use of Information Age learning tools and techniques, so they require skill building in knowledge navigation and network scholarship. Much of the coursework is redesigned into multidisciplinary subject and skill set modules that can be undertaken at the student's own pace, but in collaboration with learning teams of other students. Individual faculty mentors and seminar leaders guide the progress of individual learners.

Students begin research and problem-solving collaborations immediately after entering the program and demonstrating basic competencies. These collaborations involve current faculty in the department, other faculty at the university and at other universities around the world, graduates of the program, and distinguished practitioners and problem solvers. These collaborations are multidirectional and multidimensional.

Over time, many levels of certification of mastery of research and learning skills emerge. Students undergo rigorous examination and evaluation of research and team collaboration skills in order to receive different levels of certification. They also pay differentially for various levels of certification. Graduates and practitioners who are continuing members of the program's collaborative learning space pay for the opportunity to access special learning and research resources, develop work teams with students, and other benefits.

Learning Vignette #3

Graduate Learning as a Gateway to Perpetual Collaboration

Professor Reynolds anticipates dividing his time about equally in the coming year between the following activities: establishing basic directions for the graduate programs, mentoring the basic learning for the current students under his direction, participating in the certification of mastery for learners at various stages of study, and engaging in perpetual scholarship collaborations with graduates and practitioners. His own program of research and personal learning is shaped by these collaborations.

Learning Vignette #4
Daily Learning Sustains Teams of Knowledge Workers

Advanced Concepts, Inc., is a small, growing biomedical technology firm in suburban Washington, DC. It employs multidisciplinary teams of knowledge workers to design, market, and manufacture its products and services. These teams are perpetually shifting. They include full-time employees, consultants and temporary employees having a continuing relationship with Advanced Concepts, and strategic allies and partners.

These teams consume and process vast amounts of data and information. They generate knowledge and are the greatest source of value for the firm. Each member of the team is learning, every day, and incorporating that learning into value for the firm. Today is a typical day of work and learning.

Joanne works on the marketing plan for the team's newest product, a refined version of a blood chemistry testing device for small laboratories. This morning, she downloads data from several proprietary databases on market composition and annual testing volume. She works with a partner marketing firm that investigates

the impact of lifestyle and age on the future demand for blood chemistry studies. To help them resolve several issues, they contact the research clearing-house at the gerontology center of a major university. They are directed to several faculty members for guidance and a three-way conference call is scheduled for tomorrow. Late in the day, Joanne e-mails a proposal for a collaborative learning project to her mentor at the university where she undertook graduate studies. Tonight, she is scheduled to work in an on-line collaborative workspace regarding a paper she and two colleagues are presenting at a regional conference on health care reform.

Bill is a new engineering graduate on the team. As part of his terms of employment, he spends two hours a day engaged in on-line learning in advanced manufacturing techniques for biomedical equipment. In time, he will mentor several of the manufacturing technicians who will be applying these techniques to the new product. Bill is also investigating a new approach to the advanced circuitry in the product, in collaboration with a senior engineer at Advanced Concepts and several consultants. Tonight he will spend several hours exchanging ideas with engineering graduates from his alma mater who have formed a continuing work group on issues of interest to them.

Carolyn is the internal legal specialist for the firm. She works with the team to explore the potential exportation of the device to several international markets. She spends the morning searching the on-line records of legal and product restrictions in the countries of interest, using guidance from an expert in international barriers to product roll-out. Next week she is scheduled to participate in a two-day video conference on international marketing in the biomedical industry, sponsored by the business school of a major university.

Team members post notes about what they have learned on the team bulletin board and in the working papers for the project. The team learning budget is an integral part of the business plan for developing the new product.

M ichael begins his serious network scholarship as a junior in a first-rate high school in California. His interest and skills in computer graphics place him beyond the mentoring capacity of his teachers. Using his high school Internet account, he posts a request for advice on a special interest bulletin board. Two students from MIT respond and an intensive late-night dialogue ensues for two weeks. A three-month application of the suggestions leads Michael to realize that mastering computer-based "morphing" techniques is key to his progress.

His mentors at MIT help him realize that he must master calculus to master morphing. But it is already midterm so he cannot enroll in calculus either in high school or at the local community college. So he revisits the Internet, where he discovers a mentor at Georgia State University and another at Dartmouth College. At their suggestion, he acquires the software package Mathematica and several math and graphics tutorials. He is now positioned to seek and receive mentoring from a calculus teacher at his high school. That collaboration stimulates the calculus teacher to incorporate the use of Mathematica and an exercise in morphing into his own calculus offering for the following term.

Next year, Michael plans to work part-time for a local graphics firm, pursuing calculus studies at the local state university, and exploring alternative methods for synthesizing graphic images of large data sets.

Learning Vignette #5

Network Scholarship Begins Before College

The Four Components of Transformation

Technologically, these hypothetical learning vignettes are possible today. Higher education has encountered the leading edge of the world of Information Age learning. We are in the midst of a multitude of transitions to that new world. How can educators and institutional leaders develop visions for learning opportunities in the Information Age and organize these transitions on the pathway to genuine transformation? Exercising such transformative leadership must begin with an understanding of the process of transformation.

Transformation is not a purely linear process, but rather, four interlocking subprocesses: 1) realigning higher education with the Information Age; 2) redesigning higher education to achieve this realigned vision; 3) redefining the roles and responsibilities within realigned, redesigned higher education; and 4) reengineering organizational processes to achieve dramatically higher productivity and quality. A certain level of clear strategic thinking and fundamental realignment must precede and shape the processes of redesigning, redefining, and reengineering. However, all four components eventually will be working simultaneously.

These four processes are interconnected, perpetual, and mutually reinforcing. Understanding their characteristics can illuminate the pathways to transformation, thereby enabling educational leaders to redirect campus planning processes and resources to transformative ends. ⟳

4

Realigning with the Information Age Environment

- The Changing Nature of Information, Knowledge, and Scholarship

- The Needs of Individual Learners

- The Changing Nature of Work and Learning

o objective observer will deny that the environment for higher education has changed and that institutions have responded in a variety of ways. But many educators have acted as though the only changes in the environment have been in the availability of resources and eroding public support caused by difficult economic times. They have failed to grasp the profound significance of the demands of the Information Age and their impact on the fundamental patterns and cadences of learning. To transform higher education, we must realign it with three conditions: 1) the changing nature of information, knowledge, and scholarship; 2) the needs of individual learners; and 3) the changing nature of work and learning.

These realignments are critical to meeting the learning challenges of the 21st century. They require us to reconsider all of our basic conceptions and metaphors for how, when, and where learning occurs and the roles of providers and facilitators of learning.

The Changing Nature of Information, Knowledge, and Scholarship

As the Information Age progresses, information in all of its forms is increasing nearly exponentially. In many cases, its shelf life is shrinking correspondingly. To operate successfully in this changing environment, organizations in every sector of society are changing their basic philosophy of how they collect, process, synthesize, manage, and control information. Colleges and universities that do not accommodate changes in the use of information in learning may find themselves supplanted by more facile providers. There are several specific manifestations of this trend.

Information explosion

Almost every academic discipline is bending under the weight of more and more information. It is becoming increasingly difficult within our traditional course and degree structures to produce graduates who are competent critical thinkers, know enough about selected specialties, and

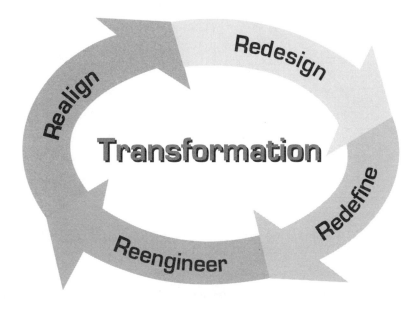

have the capacity to continue to learn and navigate to obtain information germane to their needs. Even those who succeed in achieving these goals must substantially retool themselves in three to five years. The cycle is shortening all the time and must be repeated continually throughout a productive lifetime—which by the early 21st century could mean an average life span of 90 years and an active working career into the 70s and even beyond. This could result in 10 or more complete relearning cycles throughout a lifetime.

In spite of the information explosion and educational innovation, the use of information and dissemination in learning remain fundamentally unchanged in most settings. Faculty use some technology tools to facilitate the efficiency of existing learning models, not to transform them.

The traditional classroom remains the overwhelming focal point for learning. In many classroom settings, faculty are still functioning as "talking heads" and students are passive learners. Attempts to introduce active approaches to learning have been successful, but are incremental, by and large. The classroom forum is too often used to disseminate information and not to explore implications and higher-order issues. In order to be certified as having learned, students must be associated, either physically or remotely, with classroom settings in which information is distributed.

This model does not meet the needs of the Information Age. To deal with the information explosion, the learning system must continue to evolve and expand beyond the classroom. For

Network Scholarship on Today's Campuses and in the Future

Type of Scholarship	Current Impact of Network Scholarship	Potential for Network Scholarship
Discovery Research	Revolutionizing the conduct of discovery research in some disciplines.	Discovery research and collaboration will be largely on-line. Virtual laboratories and collaboratories will abound. Findings will be presented on-line, just-in-time.
Synthesis	Revolutionizing the synthesis of findings from discovery research in scientific disciplines. Radically altering timeframe and mode of dissemination and discussion.	Synthesis of research findings will be on-line. The synthesizer's role will be accorded greater importance than today. Greater cross-disciplinary synthesis will be possible.
Teaching	Only indirectly improving teaching. Basic mode and timeframes of teaching are unaffected.	Teaching will be transformed by network scholarship. All disciplines will be affected—both at their core and in their relationships to other disciplines.
Improvement of Practice	Only indirectly affecting the improvement of practice. In many disciplines, there is a disconnect between academic research and the needs of the profession.	Network scholarship will enhance the improvement of professional practice. Knowledge workers will fuse work and learning. Perpetual learning will fundamentally affect professional practice.

example, the network can provide for distribution of basic information to be absorbed, and the seminar room—or virtual seminar space—will be the site for discussion and debate of higher-order issues informed by earlier network learning.

Network scholarship

In their scholarly and research pursuits, faculty are increasingly using network scholarship effectively to deal with the information explosion and shrinking cycle of change. The debate over cold fusion research was framed, waged, and settled over the ARPANET/Internet in a period of months, rather than the years that would have been required under traditional modes of scholarly communication. Researchers are establishing bulletin boards, "virtual laboratories," "collaboratories," and other means of sharing equipment, findings, and ideas in real time.

Network scholarship is an apt metaphor for this development—the network can be a research lab, a forum for debate, and a new venue for testing and disseminating ideas. Network scholarship increases the "bandwidth" of information that can be synthesized by an individual and shortens the timeframe. Faculty in scientific disciplines have enthusiastically embraced network scholarship for discovery research and synthesis of new knowledge. However, some faculty in disciplines where information explosion and

timeliness are not as critical as in the sciences are stuck in yesterday's model of scholarship: print media and leisurely timeframes for debate and discussion.

Using Ernest Boyer's four-part typology of scholarship, the figure on page 24 traces the current and potential impacts of network scholarship.

The tools of network scholarship are revolutionizing discovery research and the synthesis of information in particular academic disciplines. They have not been applied as successfully or thoroughly to other forms of scholarship—teaching/learning and improving professional practice. Network scholarship has the potential to shift the focus of learning from the classroom and fundamentally change what goes on in the "classroom" settings that remain. It has even changed the metaphor for the digital library of the future, which has become a distributed set of resources in a variety of physical locations that are made available through the network. The network has become the library.

Some professional disciplines are plagued by a widening gulf between the pace of change in the practice of the profession and in academic scholarship and teaching. These gaps are highly dysfunctional for the discipline and society. Network scholarship could narrow those gaps and provide a basis for dialogue between research, practice, and learners. It also provides for a two-way flow of information between scholarship and practice that could be highly beneficial and provide a continuing revenue stream for network scholarship intermediaries, such as the colleges and universities of today.

By making learning possible at any time or place, network scholarship is a liberating instrument for learners at all stages in their careers.

Information synthesis

A symptom of information explosion is the inevitable, increasing importance of a learner's capacity to continually synthesize vast amounts of information. Until recently, educators found it sufficient to distinguish between "data" and

Knowledge
(cognition)

Information
(communication)

Data
(computation)

The Creation of Knowledge

"information" — interpreted data that has a directed use. Today, a further value must be stipulated—knowledge, which is the perspective and insights that derive from the synthesis of information. Learners need to develop the capacity to search, select, and synthesize vast amounts of information to create knowledge. Given the time cycle for information change, this synthesis must

be a continuous process. This skill set is critical to success in Information Age organizations, and it must become a fundamental skill set of learning environments.

Information synthesis is not only practiced by individuals. Information synthesis by working groups is one of the key sources of value in the knowledge-driven organization. Many Information Age organizations are coming to realize the value of this knowledge and will invest in sustaining knowledge-building processes. These processes must be continually supported by just-in-time learning by individuals acting on behalf of the group.

Knowledge navigation

Many of the applications of technology in support of learning have been designed to make the factory model more efficient or more fun. Some of our educational institutions have succeeded in creating the type of learning environment required for the Information Age, but not enough.

Information Age learners need to be genuine "knowledge navigators" who develop the capacity to negotiate a pathway through an overwhelming universe of information on their way to understanding. This will require identifying, culling, and synthesizing data and information into knowledge, and capturing the results. Students will require the assistance of both human and electronic facilitators of this knowledge navigation. Knowledge navigation skills should be acquired earlier and earlier in a learner's career and continued throughout a productive lifetime. In the future, most students will bring substantial knowledge navigation skills with them from secondary school. These can be further honed at the university, or at their place of work.

The Needs of Individual Learners

An essential characteristic of learning in the Information Age is that it be highly individualized. Learning needs to occur at the time, place, and pace of the individual's choosing. This individualized character of learning will need to be established early in the learner's career and to be continually recalibrated to meet changes in the learner and the environment.

From provider-driven to learner-centered

The factory model is constructed around the needs and preferences of the providers. The campus enables the clustering of faculty, whose energies can be directed toward research, instruction, or public service. Academic calendars are designed to bring order to the delivery of courses and to provide milestones for measuring outputs. Progress for the learner is measured by grades received, courses or credit hours accumulated, degrees earned, and so forth. For the provider,

the factory model provides the metrics of management. Workload is measured in units taught per term. Productivity—and even quality—is measured by student/faculty ratio. The economics of higher education have been built upon these metrics.

The Information Age model requires a shift from a provider-driven to a learner-centered metaphor. The focus must be on responding to the needs of different learners. Not just different types of learners, but different individual learners. In the Information Age, learners will expect to be in the driver's seat if they are to get where they need to go—albeit with some navigational assistance.

Self-paced

The factory model for education establishes a set time for achieving learning objectives—from class meeting to class meeting, during a semester, or four to five years to a degree. The academic calendar, in turn, is established to fit a factory model for learning. These frameworks just do not accommodate the realities of many learners.

In a network learning environment, in which learning can occur in many ways and settings and at any time, the time to attainment of set learning objectives can vary dramatically from person to person. Ability may not be the only determining factor; highly motivated learners of average ability can outpace more intelli-

Individualized Learning

Provider-Driven, Set Time for Learning

gent but less disciplined learners. The learning objectives themselves can even vary for individual learners within an established universe that may itself be open to negotiation. Self-paced learning is essential to breaking the lock-step metaphor for learning.

Personal best

In current educational practice, most learning is based on a "minimum attainment" standard for mastery. Students are graded on their ability to absorb and be tested on a pre-established set of knowledge in particular subject areas. In a network-learning, self-paced environment, learners could navigate beyond the minimal set of knowledge to establish their own "personal best" in a particular subject area or in personalized, interdisciplinary topical areas designed in consultation with a faculty mentor(s) or in collaboration with research partners, potential employers, or other stakeholders.

New concepts and standards of personal best will also be needed to deal with the skills of advanced practitioners. These avid learners will be continually refurbishing their skills, both in areas where they have substantial expertise and in new sectors where they may well be quick studies.

Variable styles

Our understanding of differences in how individuals process information and learn

is growing rapidly. At the present time, there are many promising pilot programs in K-12 schools that are tailoring learning to the styles of individual learners using a number of multiple intelligence models. Experts expect the 1990s to witness many advances in cognitive science. Once we break the classroom-bound, lock-step metaphor for learning, we can begin to customize learning to the different learning styles of individuals.

The use of variable learning-style models will be greatly facilitated by the application of information technology. New systems of learning management will enable faculty to mentor the development of individual learner styles and to track performance.

Simulation

Computer-based simulation is one of the most powerful learning tools ever developed. In colleges and universities across the nation, such simulations are modeling everything from basic laboratory experiments to complex experimental relationships. Simulations of complex social systems are a fundamental tool in many disciplines. Can anyone imagine teaching urban geography without SimCity? Or calculus without Maple or Mathematica? Or economics without econometric and behavioral modeling?

In discovery research settings, simulation has already proven transformative. Simulation has enabled researchers to

The Power of Individualized Learning

Industrial Age	Information Age	Result of Transformation
Provider-driven	Learner-driven	Responds to the needs of individual learners.
Set time for learning	Self-paced	Learning objectives and pace are individualized.
Minimum attainment standard	Personal best	Establishes a higher targeted competence. Develops new, personalized, interdisciplinary topic areas in consultation with learning mentors.
Computer-based simulation as a classroom support tool	Simulation replaces many types of research and laboratory work, becomes a critical tool in knowledge seeking.	Dramatically improves the quality of instruction and its capacity to generate interest. Reduces cost, change mix and use of facilities.

greatly compress the time needed to conduct research iterations dealing with biological and other physical systems—also enabling the elimination of some nasty environmental issues associated with biological experimentation as well. Networked supercomputing has created research platforms for simulating phenomena that cannot be physically imagined or produced. The potential is so great that nine Federal agencies are coordinating their digital science efforts to solve roughly 30 Grant Challenges—projects that are beyond the capacity of any single researcher or lab. These challenges cover an important group of fields: computational biology, mathematical combustion

modeling, quantum chromodynamics modeling, and global climate modeling, to name a few.

In settings where it has been effectively applied, simulation has greatly reduced the cost of instruction—and dramatically improved its quality and capacity to inspire interest. It has significantly reduced our requirements for expensively configured laboratories and has thereby shaped designs for new campus facilities.

In instructional settings, simulation can decouple laboratory and other learning experiences from the time-and-place tyranny of current instructional methods. As it becomes applied more substantially, simulation can be a key ingredient in the personalizing of learning experiences and in the synthesis of information.

The Changing Nature of Work and Learning

In the transition to the Information Age, the nature of work, organizations, and learning—and the relationships among them—are in a state of flux.

The death of the job and the emergence of the knowledge worker

The concept of the "job" is a creation of the Industrial Age, during which the job evolved into a tightly defined position with a fixed set of specific responsibilities within a larger organization. Today, at the dawn of the Information Age, employers are seeking individuals who can learn, apply information and knowledge, deal

A New World of Work and Learning

	Industrial Age	Information Age
Nature of Jobs	Tightly defined positions within an organization	Knowledge workers who are mobile
Nature of Organizations	Rigid, formula-driven	Fast, fluid, flexible
Source of Organizational Value	Physical assets	Intellectual assets, group-centered knowledge
Pattern of Learning	Time out for training	Fusion of work and learning
Competitive Advantage for Education	Virtually exclusive teaching franchise. Clustering of instructional resources is a major competitive advantage.	Network scholarship, the measurement of competence, and certification of outcomes establish competitive advantage.
Defining Educational Roles	Provider	Facilitator, knowledge navigator, and learner/service intermediary

with uncertainty, and solve problems. These workers will serve organizations through a variety of relationships—such as continuous or temporary employees, consultants, or alliance partners. This new breed of "knowledge workers" is essential to Information Age organizations. While American higher education has proven highly adept at serving the needs of the Industrial Age, many observers of the academic scene conclude that it has not yet shifted to Information Age standards.

Fast, fluid, flexible organizations

The transition from the Industrial to the Information Age involves transitions from rigid, formula-driven organizations and industrial models to organizations that are fast, flexible, and fluid. Whatever organizational metaphors apply—shamrock organizations, network organizations, inverted pyramids, and a myriad of other shapes and forms from the defined to the amorphous—we know that they will require knowledge workers who have the capacity to continually retool themselves with minimal direction from the organization. These self-correcting, self-adapting, self-improving knowledge workers will require ubiquitous learning networks of great power and capacity.

New patterns of learning

Information Age learning networks will include substantially more learning participants, and the roles of providers

> **The Changing Nature of Work and Learning**
>
> - **The death of the job and the emergence of the knowledge worker**
> - **Fast, fluid, flexible organizations**
> - **New patterns of learning**
> - **Different sources of competitive advantage**
> - **A wide range of educational intermediaries**

in the network environment can change dramatically. Under the Industrial Age model, colleges and universities and the training organizations of corporations traditionally created separate, vertically integrated organizations to impart learning. All of the factors of production were included and provided to a largely resident and essentially captive group of learners—geographically isolated learners were served by visiting faculty or remote delivery of instruction. The clustering of the factors of production on the campus was the key competitive advantage. Under this factory/physical campus model of learning, the barriers to entry were huge, and two basic classes of participants existed: providers and learners. During the Industrial Age, higher education has held a virtually exclusive franchise on teaching and certifying mastery in its core areas of interest.

Different sources of competitive advantage

In the Information Age, network scholarship will eliminate much of the advantage of vertical integration and the physical concentration of scholarly resources. Not only can learners be anywhere, they can acquire learning and knowledge from sources in any location or mixture of locations. Owning the physical facility where faculty and other expertise reside will not be a critical differentiator in the eyes of many learners. On the other hand, developing the ability to provide expertise, learning, and knowledge to networked learners will be essential. The capacity to measure demonstrated competence and to certify learning in a way that will be accepted by employers will also be a key differentiator. New learning support roles—facilitators, knowledge navigators, and learner/service intermediaries—will become increasingly important. They will also become potentially lucrative.

A wide range of educational intermediaries

Today, these new roles are being explored by a host of organizations—technology companies, community-based partnerships, multi-organization alliances, and university-based groups. Most are trying to understand how to benefit in the short run from using the emerging information highway. The most insightful are looking beyond the horizon to comprehend how to develop visions, products, and services to meet the as-yet-undefined learning needs of the Information Age.

In summary, realignment with the emerging needs of the Information Age environment is an imperative for all organizations that aspire to suceed in the 21st century. Realigned vision will drive the subsequent redesign, redefinition, and reengineering that can reshape our learning landscape.

5

Redesigning to Meet the Needs of Information Age Learners

- Reconceptualizing the Role of the Information Infrastructure

- Creating Barrier-Free, Perpetual Learning

- Offering High-Quality, Flexible Enabling Services

- Reconceptualizing Around Essential Outcomes

- Pushing Out Organizational Boundaries Using Technology

- Designing New Organizational Interfaces with Learners

- Changing the Metaphors for Realigned, Redesigned Learning Organizations

*T*he network is the fundamental organizational principle of 21st century enterprises. In considering the redesign of academe, the primacy of the network metaphor is paramount. The transition from autonomous, hierarchical educational institutions to globally networked learning organizations has profound implications for academe.

The burgeoning use of the Internet and other national and international networks is creating environments where intellectual capacity, information and knowledge bases, methodologies, and other valuables are made available to learners anywhere, anytime. While network utilization is becoming virtually universal in many quarters, academe has failed to comprehend and embrace the primacy of the network as a fundamental guiding principle for redesign. Actual utilization of networks is a decision for individual learners, faculty, and administrators. However, institutions must develop infrastructure and support mechanisms to encourage adaptation of network practices. Institutions that lag too far behind in technological capacity, infrastructure, and incentives risk being unable to participate meaningfully in network learning. Operating an educational institution in the 21st century that is not a facile participant in network learning will be analogous to operating an Industrial Age institution of higher education without lecture halls, classrooms, libraries, or research labs.

The primacy of the network metaphor to the redesigning of higher education drives several conclusions. We must reconceptualize the role of information infrastructure based on the recognition that the information infrastructure will emerge as a primary delivery mechanism for educational materials. Because the network is ubiquitous and open, higher education will not own the franchise as provider. Instead, it will compete for learners with commercial firms and other intermediaries. Competing information and learner support systems are already emerging on the commercial networks. Being learner-centered will increase their competitiveness and encourage continuing development of commercial learning

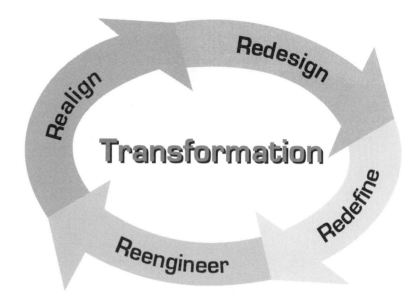

network offerings. Competitive advantage will not be established by the campus address, but by the network address. Competition will no longer be limited to other colleges and universities and some corporate training organizations, but will include global information and learner-support providers. With over 100 million new learners at stake globally, the competition will be keen indeed. As individuals, business, and government turn to network alternatives, the franchise of the college degree or college credit will face significant challenges. These challenges will stimulate rethinking of all current degree programs and structures.

Under the network learning paradigm, only world-class, relevant, appropriately priced learning offerings will survive, because learners will have many

The Network Learning Metaphor Will Dominate

▪ **All current degree programs and structures will require rethinking.**

▪ **Learners will have many choices.**

▪ **Only world-class offerings will thrive.**

▪ **Highly focused institutions will succeed in network learning.**

Information Infrastructure as the Fundamental Instrument of Transformation

Information Infrastructure as Support Tool

choices. This does not mean that the largest, most prestigious institutions will necessarily be the most successful virtual universities. Smaller, more focused, more nimble institutions may be able to craft world-class, on-line learning materials for wide use. And other learning intermediaries may tap the academic resources at our major universities to create learningware for virtual learning settings across the globe.

In addition to reconceptualizing the role of information infrastructure, other redesign changes should: reconceptualize the organization around essential outcomes, push out the organization's boundaries using technology, and design new organizational interfaces with learners.

These changes will require accepting the new metaphors about learning for the Information Age. The redesign will affect all aspects of our colleges and universities.

Reconceptualizing the Role of the Information Infrastructure

In the educational model developed for the Industrial Age, information technology has been an important ingredient in increasing the efficiency and timeliness of administrative operations. It has proven to be essential, even transformative, in the conduct of discovery research and synthesis of new knowledge. But information technology has only marginally improved instruction and learning. It has mainly been used to extend the physical reach and efficiency of our current, classroom-centered, seat time-based, teaching-focused model of learning. Taken as a whole, American higher education's investment in information technology has disappointed academic leaders. And it has failed to yield the sorts of productivity gains that have resulted from corporate investments in information technology. At least until now.

Under the emerging vision for learning in the 21st century, information technology is a primary instrument of transformation. It is the key ingredient making feasible a network learning, distance-free, knowledge navigation-based vision for the Information Age learner. The information infrastructure must be reconceptualized and viewed as an essential investment for the Information Age, not as just another competitor for scarce resources.

Assimilate and disseminate information at a far faster rate

The accelerating pace of change in information has speeded up the assembly line of knowledge. Higher education's factory model cannot accommodate this development. Learners need to cultivate the capacity to routinely screen and assimilate greater amounts of information more rapidly. A knowledge navigation model is the only workable approach.

Information must span a wider range of disciplines

Today's accountant, or environmental engineer, or microbiologist, or urban geographer requires access to and understanding of an expanding cone of knowledge in order to confront and solve everyday professional problems. Practicing professionals must access specialized and generalized information from a wide variety of disciplines. This level of information availability is the lifeblood of network scholarship. All four levels of scholarship are affected: 1) discovery research, 2) synthesis of new knowledge, 3) transmission of new ideas through teaching, and 4) improvement of the profession.

Learners must master the use of the information infrastructure far earlier in their academic careers

The knowledge network experiments currently underway in K-12 settings across the country assure that information highway-savvy students will soon be arriving on campus. This is a development that higher education must encourage. Indeed, it provides an opportunity to serve the needs of learners far earlier in their learning careers and to establish a service relationship that will literally continue for a lifetime.

In the not-too-distant future, secondary students will be regularly interfacing with university-based network scholarship long before their college years. They will

Information Infrastructure Facilitates the Emergence of the Information Age Learner

Industrial Age Learners	*Information Age Learners*
Assimilate a specified, delimited collection of information.	Screen and assimilate vastly larger collections of information.
Focus on clearly defined academic disciplines or multidisciplines.	Understand an expanding cone of knowledge covering a wide variety of disciplines.
Come to college and university with needs for remediation and skill development.	Arrive on campus with a digital portfolio of work and well-developed knowledge navigation skills.
Technology systems support and augment, but do not transform, learning.	Powerful 21st century information technology infrastructure facilitates learning transformation.
Technologies are distinct and fragmented.	Fully integrated technologies create synergy.

arrive on campus—for those who choose to enroll on campus—with a digital portfolio of work and well developed knowledge navigation skills. Since there will be wide variation in the developed skills of students, colleges will need to personalize and tailor skills development.

Technology Synergies

Individual Technologies

Technology systems must be continually enhanced to keep pace

Current technology systems in higher education are totally inadequate to the needs of knowledge navigating learners in the Information Age. On many campuses, the basic network infrastructure is in place to take advantage of the information superhighway and to accept new advances, such as wireless connections. But by tomorrow's standards, today's academic and administrative software, enabling systems software, and learning-ware are inadequate both in concept and implementation.

Educational transformation can be facilitated through a wide range of information technology-based products and services. Examples include everything from academic mail and bulletin boards to personalized systems of instruction to in-house text synthesis and publishing on demand. Much of our capacity to transform higher education is thwarted until the next generation of these products and services is in place. A transformative vision of learning in the 21st century is necessary to drive and shape these developments.

Generating the supporting technology to fulfill the promise of learning in the 21st century will require vision, substantial effort, and considerable investment of resources. Technology systems will require continual enhancement to keep pace. New mechanisms must be found to pay for this technology investment.

Technology synergies must be achieved

"Technology synergies" occur when different technologies are combined and achieve greater impact than the sum of the individual parts. To date, we have failed to systematically achieve such synergies in American higher education. However, the next generation of technologies has the capacity to fulfill this promise.

To achieve these synergies will require a technology infrastructure consisting of three layers:

Layer 1: Ubiquitous networking. This will consist of voice, data, and video telecommunications networks, anchored by cable, fiber, and/or microwave linkages.

Layer 2: Enabling operating systems and facilitating applications. In reality this may be more than one layer of systems and facilitating applications. These layers will enable networks to serve as powerful applications platforms supporting point-of-sale payment for the exchange of intellectual property. These capabilities include fully integrated academic/administrative systems, client/server-based applications, powerful smart card systems, object-oriented customer service systems, development tools, and enhanced input/output capabilities—such as information kiosks, workstations, personal digital assistants, notebook computers, and knowledge navigators.

Layer 3: Powerful learning and collaborative applications. These applications provide the muscle of transformation, but require the first two layers to be successful. They include individual digital portfolios, personalized systems of learning and learning management, interactive multi-media learning tools, knowledge navigation tools, and text/video customization-on-demand.

These layers of infrastructure create the foundation for technology synergy and transformative approaches.

For example, point-of-access services and payment will be made possible by the synergistic combination of universal smart cards, ubiquitous networks, and fully integrated, interoperable information systems operating in client/server environments. These systems will empower learners on- and off-campus. They will be part of national service networks, not stand-alone, campus-based systems. The smart cards will be useable at local merchants, for telephone use on- and off-campus, and as credit or debit cards wherever learners might be. These card-accessed systems will enable learners to reach into the knowledge network for any type of academic services; and to be reached for "intrusive" advising and reporting on academic performance at any time. Using smart cards to access networks will apply the information

Information Technology-Based Transformation Opportunities

- Academic mail
- Academic bulletin boards
- Direct electronic learning and teaching
- Digital cash/electronic purses
- Networked, electronic classrooms
- Executive information systems, decision support systems
- FAX mail, FAX on demand
- Group work space and collaboratories
- In-house text synthesis and publishing on demand
- Information kiosks
- Knowledge navigators/electronic agents
- Multimedia learning systems
- One-card systems
- On-line advising
- Personalized system of instruction
- Student retention and intervention systems
- Touch-tone registration

contained on the cards to enhance the power of integrated information systems. Smart cards will provide a level of security and control not now available. This will enable the solving of problems which the systems could not handle alone.

The investment must be used to generate additional sources of revenues to pay for the technology platforms and applications that will make them possible.

In the Industrial Age model for higher education, educational leaders did not

Synergy Creates New Opportunities

Smart Card Systems

Fully Integrated
Information
Point-of-Access
Systems and
Client/Server
Exchange and Payment
Learning
Technology
for Academic Services
Applications

Ubiquitous Networking

These systems must be a priority investment if the academy is to survive

Creating a networked learning environment depends on these sorts of systems. In the past, technology has been a capital expenditure for colleges and universities. Through dedicated state appropriation, the largesse of technology companies, philanthropy, and commitment of scarce resources, campuses developed a baseline technology infrastructure. But this model has been difficult to sustain in the 1990s, especially for the average institution.

In order to reach out to the legions of learners created by the Information Age, higher education should conceive of information technology as an investment.

need to be highly imaginative in revenue planning. Learners were operating under a set time-driven model for payment, which greatly restricted access, favored the bundling together of services, and required payment of fixed tuition. In the Information Age, educators must discover ways to increase access to legions of perpetual learners, unbundling services so that learners pay only for what they use. Institutions must also realize the revenue potential from campus-based learning services that can be sold to expanded, parallel communities of learners. Case in point: Publishing-on-demand based on a campus can serve local colleges, K-12 schools, community groups, and businesses. This can yield substantial income.

Taken together, these approaches will dramatically increase higher education revenues. These revenues can form the basis for the investment in technology necessary to achieve transformation.

Creating Barrier-Free, Perpetual Learning

In the Industrial Age model, colleges and universities have carefully established prerequisites to and conditions for learning. Students must be thoroughly screened and controlled to manage the inputs to the learning process and thereby maintain institutional quality. Indeed, one of the selective college's major functions is its ability to identify, screen, attract, and enroll high-quality students. Participation in learning is only through prescribed, time-specific patterns of courses and degrees, and more recently, through contract learning with organizations requesting precise learning specifications.

A new design model is essential to meet the needs of the Information Age. Barriers to learning must be replaced with mechanisms to facilitate: 1) open access, to 2) a network of experts, in 3) both traditional and hybridized disciplines, using 4) just-in-time learning, providing 5) perpetual learning, facilitated by 6) automated, "fused" learning systems, and 7) unbundled learning experiences based on learner needs.

Open access

In the main, today's colleges and universities are open only to learners who have been admitted to the institution for specified programs of study. Research and community service partners participate through carefully controlled relationships negotiated one at a time. Under this model, the campus boundary can become a relatively impermeable membrane.

In tomorrow's learning and knowledge navigation network, institutions will serve not only a traditional, residential population of learners, but a heterogeneous assemblage of off-campus learners, researchers, and community problem solvers. Learners will access campus networks from a complex selection of access points—information

Technology Infrastructure Is Key to Transformation

- Technology infrastructure is an investment.

- This infrastructure is essential to transformative learning services.

- Transformative learning services will yield enhanced productivity, cost savings, and new revenues.

- These learning services will generate revenues not only from postsecondary learners, but also from other sources.

- New revenues can pay for much of the technology infrastructure investment.

kiosks, personal computers, point-of-sale stations, personal digital assistants, learning "appliances" in the home entertainment center, company networks, or other locations/access points. At any point in time, the number of off-campus learners will vastly outnumber on-campus learners. Off-campus clients will access individual faculty, learning resources, virtual laboratory equipment, and other resources through carefully facilitated mechanisms. Many of an institution's alumni will remain active, loyal perpetual learners, connected through the network.

Tomorrow's campus membrane will be more permeable to a greater number of off-campus participants. But the terms and conditions of most of these relationships will need to be self-regulating and self-correcting. Establishing contractual relationships and recognizing intellectual property rights, screening of participant needs, and facilitation of proper linkages will need to be achieved with greater flexibility and facility than today. Mechanisms for screening contacts and linkages will be essential. The knowledge navigation skills of external learners, researchers, and

New Paradigm

Advanced Learning

Old Paradigm

problem solvers will need to be developed *and* facilitated for an appropriate fee.

Networked experts

Tomorrow's learning institution will be part of a network of experts—faculty, researchers, and adjunct consultants affiliated with the network. The network will be available to serve anyone, but under carefully predetermined conditions and screens. Expertise will be available for learning, discovery, and problem solving. Knowledge and intellectual property will flow freely—but in most cases not for free—among campuses and between the expert network and learners, researchers, and problem solvers. Facilitating the navigation of this network of experts will be a critical skill set for campus intermediaries who will assist learners and problem solvers. These networks of experts will be shaped by market forces acting to address clear societal needs.

Hybrid disciplines

The combination of individualized learning and networked expertise will create the capacity for learners to reshape disciplines to fit societal and/or individual needs. Leadership of the creation of new disciplines will pass from the faculty alone to faculty and learners acting collaboratively. This hybridization—even personalization—of disciplines will become a lifelong process for Information Age learners.

In the Industrial Age, the paradigm for professional education and training was a pyramid. Learners began with a broad liberal arts education at the undergraduate level and became increasingly specialized through professional and graduate training, culminating in a professional, doctoral, or post-doctoral degree or certificate. With moderate annual upgrading, the professional could maintain the competitive edge throughout his/her career.

The Information Age will continue to need highly focused specialists who perpetually upgrade their specialties. During the transition to the Information Age, many leading-edge organizations are finding that a smaller number of networked specialists can replace numerous, physically distributed specialists. This is already occurring in professional services and consulting firms, health care organizations, and other market-driven settings. However, in a mature Information Age setting, the overall numbers of specialists are likely to grow, as more and more knowledge workers require access to the skills of specialists to leverage their work efforts. Moreover, the information explosion and pace of change have greatly expanded the need for knowledge navigation skills among these specialists. Additional dramatic changes in many professional and scientific fields may require these specialists to undertake substantial changes in their orientation and skill

Changing the Distribution of Expertise

■ **Makes highly focused, narrow specialists easily available through networking.**

■ **Gives broadly educated problem solvers access to networked information, knowledge, and expertise.**

sets—witness the ongoing changes in the health care field. Specialists will need to support more effectively applied and multidisciplinary work. These changes will be greater in frequency and scope than in the past. Perpetual skill upgrading will soon be a reality in these fields.

What the Information Age needs in much greater numbers are broadly educated problem solvers who can acquire and apply knowledge in a wide range of ever-changing hybrid disciplines. In blunt terms, the Information Age may demand the primacy of the broad-based liberal arts education. For example, the physical metaphor for these professionals is not a pyramid, but an inverted, truncated cone, beginning with a broad base of critical thinking skills and expanding upward within the cone, driven by the analytic and problem-solving needs of a rapidly evolving environment. The cycle of re-invention of one's hybrid discipline will be never-ending.

Our graduate and professional schools are highly skillful in producing specialists of various kinds. However, broadly edu-

Just-in-Time Learning

Time Out for Education

cated and perpetually learning problem solvers are what the Information Age economy needs in great numbers. Our colleges and universities must transform to meet these sets of needs, based not on their preferences but on societal requirements.

Just-in-time learning

Our current learning model slices learning into predetermined components (courses) of set times (semesters), leading to certification (degree). It is based on the assumption that learning must occur in certain fundamental blocks based on seat-time and credit-hour accumulation. The current model was developed at a time when the shelf life of that learning could carry learners through a substantial portion of their careers. Even though most academics understand the shrinking shelf life of learning, the basic model has been fundamentally undamaged.

In the Information Age, these assumptions no longer hold. Network scholarship and knowledge navigation enable learning to occur in modules of any size and at any time and place. Moreover, it will be necessary for learners to repeat or upgrade many types of learning throughout their professional careers, on ever-shortening timeframes.

These developments argue in favor of just-in-time learning, the delivery of learning just before it is needed by students or practicing professionals. Some standardized, just-in-time learning modules can be carefully designed and delivered to learners all over the nation, or the world. Others can be self-constructed from available knowledge navigation tools. Effective just-in-time learning will enable a reconsideration of many of the patterns and cycles of academic life.

For example, the information explosion has increased the pressure for prolonging the time and credit hours required to complete a baccalaureate degree in many professional fields. However, the capacity for knowledge navigation and well-defined, just-in-time learning modules may enable many fields to consider dramatically shortening the time required to develop basic critical thinking skills associated with the baccalaureate degree—to three years, or even less. Profession-specific information and even skills relating to individual, potential

Just-in-Time Learning Is Critical to Transformation

- Shortens time for initial preparation.
- Improves quality of workforce/learner connection.
- Reduces cost of learning.
- Enables the fusion of work and learning.
- Dramatically alters academic patterns.

employers could be acquired in a capstone, variable period of directed study. This study could occur at the university, on the job, or in combination. Students would pay for value added, not seat time.

Perpetual learning

The existing model provides for lifelong learning or continuing education for adults who have fulfilled their basic preparatory education. Most institutions have responded by creating separate educational divisions—extension, continuing education, lifelong learning, and the like. Positively, these divisions have proven flexible and adaptive to learner needs. Negatively, they have isolated mainstream faculty from adult learners and have in some settings been seen as "second class" activities. The terms lifelong learning and continuing education have been irretrievably associated with our past and current practices in these areas.

Perpetual learning is an apt metaphor for the opportunities created by the fusion of work and learning for knowledge workers. Such learning can occur every day, as part of knowledge workers' individual responsibilities and as part of their work within teams. Much of this learning can be directly applied to problem solving and value building for their employer, and may not require certification of mastery. Other learning may require certification of indi-

vidual or group mastery and performance. Involvement in such perpetual learning endeavors may require experienced faculty working as individuals or in teams.

Fusion of learning systems

Our existing factory model for education separates learners and learning systems into different groupings: elementary, secondary, apprenticeship training, baccalaureate, graduate, postgraduate, and continuing education. These are like separate "silos" whose boundaries are distinct. We have made these boundaries difficult to navigate. The Information Age paradigm for learning debunks our traditional assumptions regarding the characteristics of these different learners and the best ways to serve them.

In the Information Age, learning systems will be fused. The organizing principles will be "knowledge based" and "demonstrated mastery." Many of the same learning tools and learningware will be used at different stages in a learner's career and revisited in updated form for refreshing and reskilling. For example, learners in secondary school, undergraduate learning, apprenticeship, and on-the-job training may all use some of the same learningware to apply trigonometry and calculus to solving practical manufacturing problems.

Perpetual
Learning

Continuing
Education

Fused
Learning
Systems

Separate
Learning
Systems

Fused Learning Systems for the Information Age

Industrial Age	Information Age
Separate learning systems	Fused learning systems
Separate "silos" for different levels of learners	Learning tools are tailored to learning need, not level of learner
Transitions from silo to silo	Students will carry skills and portfolios throughout their learning careers (K-life)
Seat time, process, and minimum standard-based	Based on demonstrated mastery
Bureaucratic, inflexible	Flexible, personalized, and easily customized
Separations between administrative and academic systems	Fused academic and administrative systems

Unbundled
Learning
Experiences

Traditional
Courses,
Degrees, and
Academic
Calendars

Unbundled learning experiences based on learner needs

Just as learning systems must be fused, learning experiences must be "unbundled"—broken into components that fit learner needs, not the rigid boundaries of traditional courses, degrees, and academic calendars. The size and nature of these experiences can vary considerably. This unbundling is critical to satisfying learner choice in the Information Age.

Offering High-Quality, Flexible Enabling Services

Two essential ingredients in the creation of individualized, barrier-free learning are personalized, tailored services and the capacity to pay for services as they are used, based on value added concepts. These capabilities will require flexible, high-quality enabling services far beyond those currently available in higher education.

Information Age service standards

Information Age learners will no longer accept the style and level of service existing in higher education today. Instead, they will come to expect the world-class service and user friendliness standards set by service and information-brokering organizations with which they deal, such as L. L. Bean, America Online, and other Information Age companies skilled in fulfillment and customer service. Cumbersome access and usage requirements will not be tolerated by the sophisticated knowledge navigator.

Many learners and employers will be willing to pay a premium for access to learning systems deploying Information Age service standards. Therefore, commercial learning intermediaries will increasingly become involved in Information Age learning. As a result, increasingly learner-friendly applications will be developed. The increasing user friendliness of the Internet with the introduction of the World Wide Web and other innovative applications is the first glimpse of what can be expected in all technology-based learner applications.

Personal learning diagnostics

Sophisticated Information Age learners will expect to access personal learning diagnostics—tools that enable individuals to diagnose the types of learning best suited to them. These will enable learners to understand how they learn best and to tailor learning approaches and even specific courses to meet their individualized needs. These diagnostic services should be made available to learners at any point in their learning careers, starting well before they reach postsecondary education. This is one of many examples of Information Age learning services that will link higher education to the K-12 learning experience of students.

Learning and mastery certification are related, yet separable issues

Measurement of performance and certification of mastery will be essential prerequisites to Information Age learners' ability to move on to higher levels of learning endeavors. Under the current model, learning and certification of mastery are structurally combined. As learning becomes unbundled from traditional courses and degrees, new mechanisms for demonstration of mastery will emerge.

This will enable several interesting developments. First, greater explicit attention must be paid to measurement of performance and demonstration of mastery. More effective, comprehensive tools of assessment can be provided. Learners may be able to pay to have their level of mastery tested and certified at any stage in the learning process.

Second, society can decide for what purposes demonstration of mastery is required, and the value that learners and organizations will pay for that certification of mastery. Professional practitioners and other types of knowledge workers may be required to have mastery certification in order to perform certain professional duties, based on demonstration of mastery, not accumulation of continuing education units.

Third, society can decide how much and what types of learning can occur without associated demonstration of mastery. Much of the perpetual learning by knowledge workers, either individuals or as part of a team, may provide insights that directly support work, but with no required independent certifica-

Learning and
Certification
of Mastery
Become
Related, Yet
Separable
Issues

**Teaching and
Certification of
Mastery Are
Structurally
Combined**

Point-of-
Access
Payment for
Exchange of
Intellectual
Property
Based on
Value Added

**Front-End,
Lump-Sum
Payment
Based on
Length of
Academic
Process**

Seamless,
Integrated,
Open,
Comprehensive
Systems

**Collections of
Fragmented,
Narrow,
Proprietary
Systems**

tion of mastery. On the other hand, many employers may require demonstration of team mastery, based on perpetual learning of different members of the team. New roles and opportunities for higher education will abound.

Demonstration of mastery and certification of performance will create some interesting revenue opportunities for colleges and universities, testing organizations, and other learning intermediaries.

Point-of-access pay plans

Most observers of higher education technology have not focused on the importance of point-of-access pay plans for educational services. In reality, the Information Age learning revolution will be fueled and enabled by four related capabilities: 1) the ability to deliver network scholarship anytime, anyplace, and on any subject; 2) the capacity to tailor educational services to individual learner needs; 3) the ability to measure performance outcomes to certify successful completion; and 4) the ability to pass intellectual property rights and receive payment on an as-used or value-added basis.

Secure, point-of-access pay plans are essential for resolving intellectual property issues on an immediate basis. They are essential to involving the legions of part-time, perpetual learners who will be the major market in the Information Age. The capacity to use these systems

in a self-regulating, self-correcting way is essential to achieving the promise of perpetual learning.

Seamless personalized services and seamless educational systems

One word best describes the emerging vision of educational enabling services in the Information Age: seamless. Individuals must be able to easily navigate the knowledge networks between learning resources residing at different nodes. Students will need to maintain and access personal diagnostics, performance portfolios, educational plans, and other information as they progress through the educational system.

To create this seamless educational system, educational leaders will need to insist on common standards so that networks, learningware, personalized diagnostics, support services, and systems can communicate and be understood. This does not mean that everyone must use the same technical or pedagogical approach. But it does mean that proprietary systems and methodologies that lock users into a particular approach and limit future options will not work to an institution's advantage. They will not create the sort of "open systems architecture" that should be encouraged in the technology infrastructure for the Information Age.

Computing and networking went through this stage of development and maturation in the late 1980s. In the 1990s, we are witnessing an equally important set of opportunities as we develop pilot capabilities for publishing-on-demand, interactive multimedia systems, on-line learning diagnostics and student performance assessment, knowledge network navigation, and smart card systems. Educators must insist on the development of robust, open systems that can support a truly seamless educational network for knowledge navigators.

Reconceptualizing Around Essential Outcomes

The Industrial Age model was based on inputs, process, and outputs. The Information Age model must focus unrelentingly on outcomes essential to success.

Eliminate the barriers between administrative and academic systems

In most postsecondary settings, academic and administrative systems have been conceived and operated as separate entities. They interrelate at certain key junctures but are not seen as truly integrated. On many campuses, the wall between academic and administrative systems has been reinforced by separate organizational units and lines of authority for academic computing and administrative computing.

These artificial barriers must be eliminated. Faculty and academic support staff will require a new generation of software tools to support the facilitation and management of learning in the Information Age university. These powerful tools will need to seamlessly link financial, demographic, learning progress, and other records contained in the university's networked databases, on smart cards, and from other external sources.

In the past, information systems development has focused on administrative systems and academic support systems. The new frontier is "learningware"—applications for the facilitation and management of learning. This must

Just-in-Time Services and Point-of-Access Pay Plans

1 Point-of-access pay plans

2 On-line text synthesis and publishing-on-demand capabilities

3 On-line learning diagnostics and remediation

4 Student performance assessment and certification

5 Knowledge network navigation

6 Simulation-based learning capabilities

7 Modular curricula

8 On-line consultation and problem solving

9 On-line use of collaboratories and virtual laboratories

10 Student learning management, tracking, and intervention

become the focus of software support systems for the Information Age.

> **Real-Time Access, Anywhere and Anytime:**
>
> ▪ **easy access to navigate knowledge networks;**
>
> ▪ **ability to acquire digital or printed copies of learning materials;**
>
> ▪ **evaluation of individual learning styles;**
>
> ▪ **learning programs tailored to individual learning styles;**
>
> ▪ **assessment of performance; and**
>
> ▪ **certification of learning attainments.**

Eliminate time and distance boundaries

Higher education has conditioned learners to accept the aphorism, "all in good time." Today's learners are becoming impatient. Their dealings with world-class service providers in other settings have conditioned them to expect just-in-time and real-time services. Future learners will expect the same service from higher education providers. Similarly, distance must cease to be a barrier to learning, or even a factor. Learners will demand access to knowledge resources from any location. Both learning resources and learners should be conceived of as networks that are fused. Learners, faculty, and other knowledge resources should be capable of searching and being found by one another. Many productive, collaborative work groups will be formed from such searches.

Providers must understand essential outcomes

Despite the progress made by the assessment movement over the past decade, higher education still is not outcome-driven. Our educational metaphors are still based on "quality" of student and faculty inputs, seat time, and the nature of the educational process. Faculty contributions to specific outcomes are blurred by their participation in instruction, scholarship/research, and public service.

To meet the learning needs of the Information Age, we must develop a better understanding of learning outcomes. The perpetual learner will have his knowledge navigation needs satisfied by the successful collection of knowledge and application of knowledge to problem solving. This satisfaction can be measured. Many learners will continue to want course credits, degrees, and certification of various kinds. Even these will need to be modified in the face of network learning, however. Higher education will require new generations of assessment and performance measurement tools to achieve these ends.

Meeting the learning needs of society is the first priority

Learning initiatives must be shaped by the learning needs of society. In order to serve learners in the Information Age, it will be necessary for colleges and universities to change their systems and philosophies. If they do not, other learning intermediaries will secure the knowledge resources resident in universities to serve these new learners and win the marketplace.

Higher education will miss many opportunities if it fails to realign its vision with the needs of the Information Age.

Sorting out the learning needs of Information Age society will pose intriguing issues. Colleges and universities will find it necessary to decouple their various outcomes and functions, and interpret them in the context of learner needs. How much is society willing to pay for measurement and certification of mastery, and at what levels? For traditional courses and degrees, certification of mastery is an integral part of higher education's role and function. But for perpetual, fused work and learning, many learning transactions will be unevaluated or uncertified. Learning will directly support problem-solving work teams and knowledge development by the individual or team. In this capacity, learning is immediately associated with organizational value. At what point is any form of mastery measurement needed? Is it individual mastery, or group mastery?

Meeting the Perpetual Learning Needs of Society Must Be the First Priority

- ■ Colleges and universities must decouple the different outcomes of higher education.
- ■ Educators must understand essential learning outcomes, including those relating to learners in the workplace.
- ■ The learning needs of society must be our first priority.

Who pays for certification, and how much? Another interesting issue concerns society's willingness to pay for higher education's ability to screen academic applicants and judge capability. These issues will be prominent on the 21st century learning agenda.

Pushing Out Organizational Boundaries Using Technology

Technology is the instrument that will enable higher education to push out its boundaries to serve learners everywhere. A transformative learning vision is the guide to removing artificial conceptual boundaries that still constrain educators.

Bring the university to the learner

In the Information Age, many learners will still wish to be resident at colleges and universities for different stages of their learning careers. Those who choose to reside on a campus will find their academic lives changed dramatically, however. Learners will access faculty not only who reside on their campus, but anywhere on the knowledge network. Knowledge navigation tools will change the: 1) timing and focus of learning; 2) relative balance between network, seminar, and laboratory-based learning; and 3) roles of faculty, students, and support staff. Learning will be brought to the learner at many locations in the university setting, not primarily in the classroom.

The greatest impact of the knowledge network approach will be the ability to reach learners in literally any location off-campus, and at any time of the day, week, month, or year. This will increase the capacity of higher education to serve more learners—by an order of magnitude. This vision provides the promise of expanded opportunities for educators who are willing to develop new approaches to match the learning metaphors for the Information Age.

Fusion of work and learning

Time-out-for-education will be replaced by just-in-time (JIT) learning. JIT learning will enable the fusion of work and learning. It will be the predominant mode of learning in all settings, beginning at some point in most students' K-12 learning experience and continuing throughout a learning lifetime. JIT learning will enable learners to accept more responsibility on their jobs earlier in their careers and because they can secure perpetual training as they need it.

Some JIT learning will consist of carefully planned and crafted learning modules. Practitioners and professionals will work with educators to develop key JIT modules for graduating professionals. This will shorten the time required for basic education. Other JIT learning will consist of sorting through a combination of learning modules and information sources to create knowledge relating to a particular problem or project. Some JIT learning will be undertaken by individuals, either for their own use or to support a team working on a problem. Other JIT learning will be undertaken by whole teams, working collaboratively on a joint problem or project.

Reach out to network expertise

The knowledge network will be massive. It will potentially encompass all faculty at participating institutions, research institutes, and think tanks. It could also involve distinguished practitioners and experts in other settings who make themselves available for seminars, consultation, and problem solving. The demand from the universe of learners will dictate the differentiation and utilization of different types of expertise. It will require the full spectrum from abstract theory to skillful application and implementation.

Tomorrow's knowledge networks will definitely be two-way relationships. Individual or group learners who seek the guidance of an expert or faculty one day may be approached to be part of a work group involving that expert the next day. Learning networks will be an integral part of the mechanism which organizations will use to identify consultants, recurrent employees, and even full-time staff. They will also be part of the means used by independent professionals both to keep their expertise current and identify new work relationships.

Tomorrow's knowledge networks will be highly inclusive and open. But this openness can lead to overcommitment. As a result, strict standards of engagement and protocols will be developed for different types of network scholarship. Experts will carefully stipulate their terms of engagement and screen opportunities. Both electronic intermediaries and human intermediaries who serve as gate-keepers will emerge. In this environment, familiarity and proven relationships will be highly important in establishing knowledge linkages.

Achieve virtual learning

The adjective "virtual" means existing in intent and not form. It is an apt description of the learning model of the future. The primary infrastructure of virtual

> **A Massive, Just-in-Time Knowledge Network Can Develop:**
> - defined, JIT modules plus extensive capacity to develop relationships;
> - knowledge networks of faculty, researchers, and practitioners;
> - JIT applications ranging from abstract theory to skillful application;
> - two-way learning relationships; and
> - inclusive and open relationships.

learning is cyberspace, its member networks, access tools, and support mechanisms. Serving the learner who attends the virtual university are intelligent electronic agents that seek out information and retrieve it, or execute orders and acknowledge the achievement, or lie in wait on the network for an event and then act.

Agents can be powerful tools of learning in the hands of a student or scholar. Electronic agents can sift databases for the most sought after citation, trace the citation's lineage, and compile a comprehensive citation reference to aid the scholar in assessing the value of a particular piece. Electronic agents can look for important pieces of information in collateral databases (databases not normally associated with the scholars' subject matter) and bring them to the scholar

> ## Virtual Learning Will Be the Learning Model of the Future
>
> ▪ virtual—existing in intent, not form;
>
> ▪ from network adhocracy to virtual universities;
>
> ▪ networks exist today—they will be connected to each other, digitally;
>
> ▪ move from informal to formal;
>
> ▪ range from closed (membership-based) to open.

complete with explanations and background.

Electronic agents can find appropriate simulations on a subject and bring them to the scholar for use or find other virtual learners studying the same subject and assemble a virtual classroom. The students in the virtual classroom could then search for faculty (perhaps one, perhaps more) to help guide them through the subject matter of interest. In cyberspace, this can all be recorded and played back if the student needs to review or if a new faculty brought into the virtual classroom needs to review past learning activities. The virtual classroom can be attended at any time, day or night, from anywhere; network access affords the learner cyberspace opportunity.

Electronic agents and other, artificial intelligence-based learning tools will be highly useful in searching and retrieving data and information. However, the greatest value added will occur in the synthesis of information into knowledge by learners. This will require the judgment of individual learners or groups of learners. The fusion of learning and work will create many circumstances where these knowledge-building activities serve the problem-solving efforts of collaborative work teams. Indeed, cognitive scientists will likely make significant progress over the next few years in the understanding of how such efforts contribute to the intellectual base of the organization, which is the foundation for value of Information Age enterprises.

Designing New Organizational Interfaces with Learners

Today's colleges and universities interface with learners in time-honored ways that have been marginally improved by automation. Tomorrow's Information Age learner will need new interfacing mechanisms that operate in real time, with greater efficiency and adaptability. These interfacing mechanisms will be one of the fundamental facilitators of the new metaphors for learning.

One interface doesn't fit all

There will be no such thing as a "typical" learner in the 21st century. Learners will come in all shapes and sizes; at all different levels of knowledge and expertise; with different learning needs and desired levels of involvement. Interfaces must be sufficiently adaptable, flexible, and self-correcting to serve all of these different types of learners. Fused learning systems with highly adaptable interfaces will be the solution to this requirement.

Configured for the individual needs of learners

We are not yet stretching the metaphor to dream of interfaces that will be customizable to fit the needs of individual learners. Just as learners will be able to craft learning programs to fit their personal learning styles and needs, the organizational interfaces should match individual needs.

Access and security, record keeping, and control

To attain the customized, real-time, network learning environment envisioned for the 21st century, several substantial technical challenges must be overcome.

First, while access to knowledge networks must be facilitated and eased, that access must be under conditions of strict security. Access to different parts of the knowledge network and to individual data must be carefully regulated. These requirements will drive substantially greater interest in "point-of-sale" transactions—the exchange of financial value at the point of sale or distribution of a particular academic service. The password-based model of security existing in today's network environment

Functions Facilitated by Smart Cards

Smart cards become the key to access, record keeping, and control. Functions facilitated using smart cards in conjunction with networked, fully integrated information systems include:

- Advising card
- ATM card
- Building access card
- Computer access card
- Coupon/discount card
- Credit card
- Debit card
- Disbursement card
- Grade card
- Health card
- Identification card

- Learning plan/catalog card
- Library card
- Meal plan card
- Message card
- Network access card
- Parking card
- Telephone card
- Ticket/event system access card
- Transcript/student record card
- Vending card (stored value card)

is inadequate to these future needs.

Second, scrupulous record keeping must accompany point-of-access sales and transactions on the knowledge navigation network. This level of record keeping outstrips the reasonable capacity of existing information systems. New approaches are necessary to address this imperative.

Third, control of the conditions and level of access will be key to the functioning of the knowledge navigation network. Many of the participating faculty and practitioner experts on the network will wish to have their accessibility both facilitated and screened. Systems must be developed to enable such facile access and control.

Most educators and information technologists have found it daunting to even

The Campus Will Be Transformed

■ Learners will have choices—some will hold on to traditional means.

■ The classroom will not disappear, but its usage patterns will be more varied.

■ Time, place, and content boundaries will become negotiable.

■ The standards for access, security, record keeping, and control will become more rigorous.

■ Transformed colleges and universities will play a pivotal role in network learning.

envision the learning environment of the 21st century because of the magnitude of these challenges. However, the synergistic combination of smart card systems, ubiquitous networks, and integrated information systems in a client server environment holds promise as a solution.

The campus will not disappear, but it will be transformed

The relative importance of the campus in the total learning universe will change, but the campus will not disappear. Rather, it will be transformed. The traditional cycles of academic life will continue for many learners, but time, place, and content boundaries will all become negotiable.

Transformation will not affect everyone equally. The classroom will not disappear. American higher education in the 21st century will provide a variety of choices for learners, ranging from the traditional to the totally transformed. These choices will be exercised by individual learners, faculty, researchers, and practitioners in their daily work and as they chart the path of their learning careers. However, institutions that fail to provide transformative choices will miss the expanded opportunities to serve millions of additional Information Age learners. They also risk being marginalized in their capacity to compete for "traditional" learners.

Transformed colleges and universities can play a pivotal role in the network learning environment of the future. However, if higher education refuses to change, holding on with stubborn conviction to its traditional culture and practice, it will suffer lingering attrition. Limited in resources and under assault by its stakeholders, colleges and universities will find their intellectual resources cherry-picked by more nimble knowledge networking organizations. Is this the future of higher education—to provide the raw materials for more imaginative learning intermediaries? To see faculty resources become an easily available commodity, with real value being paid for facilitating learning or certification of mastery? Only if our vision fails.

There is another essential upside to Information Age learning. If higher education realigns and redesigns itself to fit Information Age needs, it will find that learning offerings are far more important and immediately consequential to individuals and organizations. Its offerings will not only develop human capital, but will also contribute immediate, perpetual value to fused work and learning environments. This is the stuff of which competitive advantage is made. Individuals and organizations will be willing to pay handsomely for such valuable contributions to their success. They will also become vocal stakeholders in support of a responsive and value-rich higher learning enterprise.

Changing the Metaphors for Realigned, Redesigned Learning Organizations

Realigning and redesigning higher education requires transformation of our basic metaphors for education. The current emphasis on teaching should be recast as a dedication to learning. Higher education must transform its concept of seat time-based education and focus on achievement-based learning. Classroom-centered instruction should begin to embrace and transition to network learning. Indeed, the network becomes the fundamental organizational metaphor for Information Age educational enterprises. Our current emphasis on information acquisition should graduate to a more sophisticated emphasis on knowledge navigation. Distance education should be replaced with distance-free education. And continuing education should disappear from our lexicon, replaced by a new notion of perpetual learning.

Fusion is an apt metaphor for the Information Age. Rather than taking time out for learning, learning and work are fused. Separate systems that serve different types and levels of learners will be succeeded by fused learning systems serving all learners, but at different levels of attainment. And products and services developed for learners in one setting can be adapted to the fused

Changing Metaphors for Realigned, Redesigned Learning Organizations

Industrial Age	*Information Age*
Classrooms, libraries, and laboratories	Network
Teaching	Learning
Seat time-based education	Achievement-based learning
Classroom-centered instruction	Network learning
Information acquisition	Knowledge navigation
Distance education	Distance-free learning
Continuing education	Perpetual learning
Time out for learning	Fusion of learning and work
Separation of learners and learning systems	Fusion of learning systems

network for broader clienteles. The revenue potentials from fused learning systems are massive—but so is the potential for competition.

Put simply, higher education cannot enter the new Learning Age until it elevates its vision, redesigns systems, and embraces new metaphors for learning.

6

Redefining Roles, Responsibilities, and Productivity

■ Faculty Roles and Responsibilities

■ Learner Roles and Responsibilities

■ Administrator Roles and Responsibilities

■ Productivity

*T*he realigned, redesigned higher education organization will have the opportunity to recast the roles of all participants. The redefinition of roles has the potential to reap substantial increases in the productivity of all participants in the learning process.

Industrial Age colleges and universities pay a great deal of attention to productivity. The "P" word is on every stakeholder's tongue—legislators, governors, parents, students, faculty, and employers. But the productivity focus is on throughput, output, workload, and resources won. These are not the productivity measures that interest Information Age learners as they differentiate between learning providers or intermediaries. Higher education must do a far better job of understanding and capitalizing on network scholarship to dramatically enhance the productivity of everyone associated with the higher education enterprise.

Productivity in the Information Age university will be measured differently. It will assess outcomes, success in meeting the needs of different types of learners, and effectiveness in addressing the needs of the range of stakeholders of higher learning. If educators display leadership and vision in responding to the needs of Information Age learners, they can enjoy increasing support from the full spectrum of publics and stakeholders.

Faculty Roles and Responsibilities

In the Information Age learning environment, however, faculty will play a variety of roles—researcher, synthesizer, mentor, evaluator and certifier of mastery, architect, and navigator. These roles will not be played in equal measure by all faculty. The Learning Age university will enable greater role differentiation and specialization. The demand for different mixes of roles for learning and other forms of scholarship will be established by the marketplace. One mode will not predominate. Over time, existing models of scholarship, faculty promotion and rewards will change in the face of these developments.

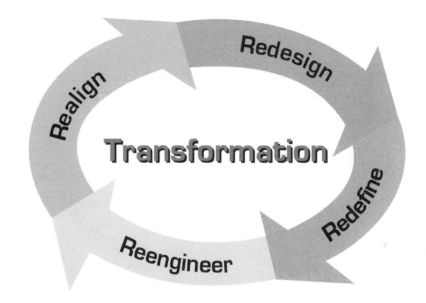

Researcher

Under today's model, discovery research and resulting publication is expected of most faculty at research universities and those institutions that emulate that model. In the future, discovery research will remain a seminal role for faculty, but it will be conducted by a smaller proportion of faculty who are truly adept at discovery. Most of those highly productive researchers will spend a large proportion of their time—even most or all of their time—involved in discovery research.

The creation of virtual research environments and network scholarship will change the manner in which research findings are tested and disseminated. The existing system of scholarly publication will be substantially revamped in the face of real-time scholarship. Change will be nurtured by: digital journals, a greater

Key Faculty Roles in the Information Age Learning Environment

■ Greater role differentiation will be possible in the Information Age learning environment.

■ Discovery research will be conducted by a smaller group of stellar researchers.

■ Synthesis will be important for all faculty at some level.

■ The term "teacher" will pass from usage. Learning mentors will help students develop higher-order cognitive skills.

■ Evaluation and certification of mastery will be a significant and rewarding role for faculty.

■ Some faculty will serve as architects in designing new curricula and learningware.

■ Faculty will serve as knowledge navigators for the learners they are mentoring. For many students, at various stages, faculty will need to serve as co-pilot.

emphasis on synthesis of discovery research findings, the development of listserves and other forums for exchange and dissemination via the Internet, and the press to get new ideas into circulation quickly. The current, publish-or-perish norm in existing academic print journals will also come under assault as the balance of faculty and graduate student effort shifts from traditional discovery research to a broader range of scholarly activities. Research and practical applications dealing with learning-related topics will spawn a new echelon of electronic jour-

nals, forums, and bulletin boards. Many learning insights will be exchanged freely and for free. In addition, the learning-ware industry will be a major source of income for educational institutions and other providers.

Synthesizer

Even today, a substantial portion of the time spent by faculty on "research" is really the synthesis of new knowledge created by others. In the face of the information explosion, the synthesis and rapid dissemination of new knowledge will emerge as an even more important position in the spectrum of scholarship. This is the point where truly monumental bottlenecks can occur, given the information explosion. Scholars will find their investment of time in synthesis of new knowledge substantially aided by electronic agents and other knowledge navigation tools that greatly reduce the time required for searching and synthesis.

Just as network scholarship will allow discovery researchers to cluster in addressing topics of interest, network scholarship will provide learners, practitioners, and other faculty with access to distinguished synthesizers of old and new knowledge. These distinguished synthesizers—typically senior faculty able to bring the perspective of an academic lifetime to the confluence of old and new developments—will be available to learners of all kinds. This will be a tremendous resource. Synthesizing sages such as Peter Drucker will be even greater global figures in networked scholarship.

Mentor

The model for mentors exists today at the graduate level in many academic disciplines, in some undergraduate settings, and in "new school" experiments in K-12 education. Over time, this model will spread throughout higher education at all levels.

Learning mentors will help students deal not with basic information on a subject, but on sorting out relationships and higher-order concepts. Preparation for mentoring sessions will include substantial knowledge navigation by the learner. Mentoring opportunities will be almost unlimited and will deal with a fascinating range of learning and problem solving.

The faculty role of mentor will also be transformed with regard to graduate students. The current research university model of graduate teaching assistants will be transitioned. Graduate students will have the opportunity to gain experience and to hone their skills in the full range of scholarship—discovery research, synthesis, learning, and improvement of practice. Graduate students will collaborate with senior faculty and instructional technologists in developing and testing learningware and different approaches to learning and problem solving. The new market demands for learning will dictate

revisions in the traditional patterns of increasingly specialized graduate training that is fundamentally designed to produce new discovery researchers.

Evaluator and certifier of mastery

In the teaching model, instruction and certification of mastery are seamlessly bundled. In the learning model, these functions will be unbundled. Many learning experiences may be unevaluated, at least until the learner requires some form of certification. At that time faculty will be called upon to assess and certify mastery of learners, many of whose learning did not occur through their personal instruction.

The certification of mastery for independent, perpetual learners may become a highly significant and rewarding role for faculty—or for other intermediaries who develop expertise in assessment. In any case, the assessment role for faculty should receive enhanced attention in the Information Age learning environment.

Architect

Faculty will also serve as architects in designing the curriculum and the learning architecture that will enable knowledge navigation by researchers, faculty, and learners. They must also specify the evaluative tools to assess performance and demonstrate when individuals have achieved mastery of particular topics. Faculty must collaboratively design the combinations of skills sets, mastery, and development that are required for awarding credit, certification, or degrees.

This future architecture will be much more complex and adaptable than today's. While it is likely that many current credit hour and degree/certificate conventions will continue—albeit in a revised, outcome-driven form—it is also clear that altogether new standards for learning will be required for the perpetual learner who is not interested in additional traditional degrees, however cleverly reengineered. The perpetual accumulation and demonstration of learning will be a substantial challenge for faculty in their roles as architects.

Faculty teams will direct teams of academic support staff who will develop knowledge navigation tools, instructional information, and other learning materials. This is a critical role, since a broadly available network of these tools will be necessary to liberate faculty from the role of "instructor," enabling them to become true "learning mentors." Academic support staff and junior faculty with an interest in learning will be in high demand.

Navigator

Faculty will serve as learning navigators for the learners whom they are mentoring. The nature of this role will vary substantially from learner to learner, especially in the early stages of transformation to the Information Age model.

Some learners will require more guidance than others.

As learning navigators, faculty will guide learners in identifying and fulfilling their learning objectives. Plans of study and learning will be tailored to individual needs and will express a healthy respect for the capacity to change plans as new needs and opportunities emerge. This role of navigator will require substantial insight on the part of faculty. It will be far more complex, challenging, and rewarding than today's model of advising students against a fixed set of catalog requirements.

In the Information Age, navigation will acquire the respect and standing that student advising has lost under the factory model of higher education.

Learner Roles and Responsibilities

Learner roles will change as dramatically as those of faculty. The term "student," which more aptly describes a pre-adult stage of life, will pass from common usage for post-adolescent learners. The primary characteristics and roles of students will include active learner, responsibility for learning outcomes, maintenance of connection and commitment to learning, and pilot.

The combination of these characteristics and roles will vary from setting to setting and from student to student.

Active learning

The learner as passive recipient of information in the classroom is an artifact of the factory model of instruction. In the Information Age, active learning will be the rule. This will be true for traditional, residential learners and for learners fusing work and learning.

Many studies of how current undergraduate students spend their time suggest that there are up to 20 hours per week, on average, that could be redirected to active learning. This is the price that is paid for having a single learning model. In an active learning, self-paced environment, some students could choose to accelerate their progress, either completing their learning in a shorter period of time, or allowing for enrichment of learning with practical experience.

For the perpetual learner, active learning will be the only acceptable style. Most learning ventures will be: 1) a specific just-in-time learning requirement; 2) part of a collaborative team project; and/or 3) tailored by an individual learner as part of a process of perpetual improvement.

Responsibility for outcomes

Learners will assume greater responsibility for their own learning outcomes in a network scholarship environment. Beginning in K-12 education, students will make learning choices, assemble performance portfolios, and focus on learning outcomes, not seat time. These habits will

Key Learner Roles in the Information Age

- Learners will assume vastly different roles based on personal choice and stage of learning.
- Active learning will be more popular at all levels.
- Learners will assume greater responsibility for outcomes at all levels. There will be great variation in patterns of outcomes and responsibilities.
- Learners will remain connected and maintain access at all stages of their learning careers.
- Many learners will become the pilots of their learning experiences. This will require new learner skill sets.

continue and grow throughout their learning career. Employers will count on permanent and temporary employees being able to maintain and expand skill levels and learning with only modest navigational assistance. These skills will be essential to the long-term economic success of learners in the marketplace.

Remain connected, maintain access

Learners in the Information Age will not be able to afford the luxury of on-again, off-again learning. They will need to remain connected to knowledge navigation networks and learning throughout their lifetime. As knowledge navigation tools are continually improved and upgraded, learners will risk missing new developments and capabilities if they are not continually "plugged in" to perpetual learning.

Pilot

Under the Information Age model, learners will pilot their own learning journeys, acquiring new skills and tools. Faculty will serve as navigators.

Clearly, this shift will require new learning skills and tools for charting learning opportunities. In the future, students will develop substantial knowledge navigation skills in high school, or even before, arriving at university with the capacity to serve as pilots of their learning journeys. Indeed, certifying knowledge navigation skills or completing networked tutorials to acquire such skills will likely be a key part of the college admission process.

Even after the initial transition to the Information Age model, however, there will be substantial variation in the capacity of individual learners to serve as their own pilots. In many cases, faculty will need to serve as co-pilots until students have acquired and proven the necessary skills.

Students should receive baccalaureate degrees from 21st century universities only after certifying their ability to participate in active learning, assume and execute responsibility for outcomes, remain connected to knowledge networks, and pilot their own learning enterprises.

Administrator Roles and Responsibilities

Administrators in the 21st century university will assume the roles of general contractor, developer, and systems operator and auditor. These roles and responsibilities will require greater imagination than in the Industrial Age. Higher education will be in competition with a broader range of learning providers and intermediaries, many of whom will have highly developed skills in customer service. In order for higher education to tap the opportunities that will exist in the early stages of the Information Age, academic and administrative leaders must exercise vision and aggressive leadership.

General contractor

Administrators will serve as "general contractors" in shaping the construction of the technology infrastructure and knowledge navigation network of the future. They will assure that the necessary participants—faculty, academic support staff, information technologists, technology vendors, and other strategic allies—are working together to flesh out the implications of the transformative vision and develop the necessary new products, services, and attitudes. Transformation cannot be imposed on the academic community—it must be embraced. Administrators will have a major role in redirecting existing academic and administrative processes to a transformative vision.

In order to become an Information Age enterprise, substantial new technology infrastructure, products, and services will need to be developed in higher education. The general contractor role is critical to this development effort, because it assures that all necessary parties are assembled and made aware of the transformative vision.

Developer

In addition to serving as general contractors, administrators must launch, fund, and oversee the development of many of the systems, products, and services for the Information Age. This will require greater vision of the next generation of products and services.

Systems operator and auditor

Administrators in the Information Age university will need to fulfill a critical auditing function. It will be necessary for them to audit the organization's responsible execution not only of financial or fiduciary responsibilities, but its stewardship of its learning support and certification role. Tomorrow's audit function will require continual monitoring of the institution's performance in serving learners in knowledge navigation, performance assessment and certification, and delivery of promised products and services.

Most importantly, administrators must always find ways to involve faculty in the transformational process. A shared vision of transformation must be developed and embraced by virtually all components of the university. This will be a substantial organizational development challenge.

Productivity

Higher education will radically redefine productivity as part of its redefinition of roles and responsibilities.

This redefinition will be part of an emerging social contract between higher education and society that will assure an even more salient role for higher education in the 21st century.

The concept of productivity must be recast for the Information Age

Our current concept of productivity is straight from the Industrial Age—based on throughput and seat time-based products such as credit hours and degrees awarded. Information Age standards must be developed that are based on learning outcomes and demonstrated capabilities.

Colleges and universities must join another movement that has become a fundamental characteristic of the Information Age: a dedication to the needs of clients or customers. Faculty will establish the standards for the demonstration of mastery of topics and the performance standards for the awarding of course credit or degree/certificate credit. However, learners will demand substantial control over the conditions and timing for the acquisition of skills and

Redefining and Enhancing Productivity

- ▪ Cost savings, downsizing/rightsizing, and restructuring have all missed the point—enhancing productivity is the end game.

- ▪ Learner needs must drive our concept of productivity.

- ▪ Variety, quality, timeliness, and responsiveness are important aspects of Information Age productivity.

- ▪ Higher education will enhance its productivity or pay the consequences.

demonstration of mastery. Separating these aspects of learning will enable the development of new paradigms.

Variety, quality, timeliness, responsiveness don't show up in current metrics for productivity

Moreover, current productivity measures for higher education do not address several issues that are critical to meeting the needs of individual customers. Variety, quality, timeliness, and responsiveness will become standard measures for the Information Age university. These measures focus on the conditions of delivery and are the domain of the customer/acquirer of learning. Educational institutions or other learning intermediaries that are most successful in meeting the delivery needs of learners will win the contest for the learning marketplace. Those that refuse to change will be left to serve only those learners who are in the traditional stages of their learning careers, seeking traditional means of education.

Expectations that higher education will enhance productivity are accelerating

At a time when every other major institution in society—corporations, health care organizations, non-profits—are enhancing their productivity as a means of controlling costs and improving service, higher education stands in stark relief. The pattern of retrenchment, reorganizing, and restructuring has not yielded substantial productivity gains within the academy—by anyone's definition. Indeed, most of the responses to fiscal crisis have carefully steered away from changing the basic metaphors for instruction and other forms of scholarship.

This focus and intensity of response cannot continue. And many of higher education's stakeholders know it. If the leadership in higher education does not chart a course for moving higher education into the Information Age, then others will attempt to chart that course for us. Or they will navigate around higher education, finding other learning agents and intermediaries who can address the opportunities attached to learning in the Information Age—and reap the rewards.

7

Reengineering Organizational Processes

- **Reengineering Administrative Processes**

- **Reengineering Academic Processes**

- **Overcoming the Mythical Barriers to Transformation**

- **Confronting the Real Barriers to Transformation**

69

*T*he last transition in the fundamental economic paradigm was the shift from the agrarian to the industrial economy. Many of the theories, practices, procedures, and organizational structures of modern management, education, and government were formulated during the period of transition and the Industrial Age that evolved. They have been modernized by 20th century improvements and by a new layer of information technology to improve their efficiency. But, at heart, they remain the vestiges of earlier times.

As we approach the shift in paradigms to the Information Age, two key lessons can be learned from the last transition. The first lesson was that some underlying technology both enables and pushes the transition. For the Industrial Age, the steam engine, internal combustion engine, and jet engine were important sequential, "pushing" technological developments. For the transition to the Information Age the emergence of computing, the fusion of telecommunications with computers, and the emergence of ubiquitous networking are "pushing" the transition to the new "information-based" economy. New generations of powerful applications will be a future driver.

The second lesson was that productivity gains require both incorporating the new technology and developing new enabling organizational structures and methods for accomplishing work.

To date, most reengineering initiatives in higher education have focused upon administrative processes. While these initiatives have developed important skills in institutions, the next generation of reengineering initiatives will be more ambitious. Their focus will extend far beyond managing student accounts, student records, financial aid, employee payroll and benefits, and campus maintenance. They will underpin and directly support the instructional process and learner services. The next generation of reengineering will help transition the organizational culture from provider-driven to learner-centered. But first the barriers created by bureaucratic cultures must be understood and overcome.

The industrial organization model led to the development and growth of the

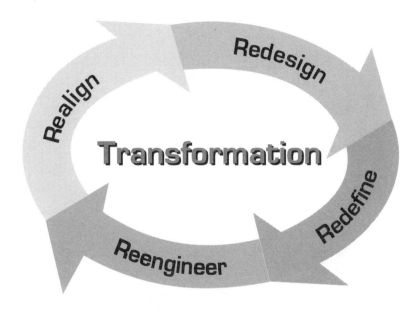

structures and procedures that came to be called "bureaucracy." The bureaucracy was created during the Industrial Age to provide command, control, and communication between organizational layers and units. It was necessitated by limitations in the capacity of Industrial Age organizations to process and disseminate information. By embedding the "rules" in tomes such as administrative manuals, organizations achieved order, maintained responsibility and established the bureaucratic culture by which the Industrial Age managed its affairs. The rules were actually well-defined prescriptions for how to handle every conceivable variation in organizational circumstance. Within the bureaucratic culture, the rules became more important than the outcomes they were designed to foster. The

Self-Informing, Self-Correcting Systems

Bureaucratic Systems

Families of Transactions Customizable to the Needs of Learners, Faculty, and Staff

Rigid, Predesigned Processes

rule book became every bureaucrat's rationale for rigid adherence to administrative routine. In its time, bureaucracy was a positive factor.

Today, bureaucracy and its culture are incompatible with an Information Age organization. In the Information Age, time is a critical competitive factor. Every possible variation in circumstance cannot be foretold. The models for providing command, control, and communication need to be recast to serve the realities of the Information Age. Rules need to be replaced by informed judgment and action. Bureaucracy needs to be replaced by self-informing and self-correcting systems.

Self-informing systems provide a means to systematically evaluate the information that resides in institutional databases to determine if intervention is necessary. Self-informing systems are invaluable when used to advance the objectives of the organization and the learner. Take student retention as an example. A self-informing system would monitor student grade performance and identify all students whose GPA fell by more than an established threshold limit, perhaps 0.2 percentage points from one term to the next. Such systems would even deal with grade and performance variations within a term/course.

Self-correcting systems use the power of system integration to act on the information. For example, the self-correcting system would automatically schedule the students with shrinking GPAs for intrusive advising, perhaps even assist in developing a corrective action plan. It would then monitor the learners' progress in meeting corrective objectives and schedule follow-up attention, as required. This level of support is not commonly available in an environment where administrative and academic systems are separate and not integrated.

One of the central insights of Industrial Age reengineering is that organizations tended to focus on functions and organizational "silos," rather than the cross-cutting processes that actually are at the heart of serving the organization's clients or customers. But in the Information Age organization, rigid, predesigned processes can themselves impede the efforts of knowledge navigating learners, faculty, and support staff. The next generation of software systems will address this issue through a variety of means, such as using families of transactions that are customizable to the needs of individuals.

These families of transactions will be bundled together by users to meet their needs for designing, acquiring, and paying for learning and the transfer of intellectual property. They will also be used by faculty, administrators, and academic staff in supporting learning and administrative activities. These transactions could be made available through on-line, object-oriented menus that would be easy to use and much more secure than existing mechanisms.

Reengineering Administrative Processes

During the early stages of transition to the Information Age, institutions have failed to achieve anticipated productivity gains from the use of information technology. The failure is widely recognized and lamented. The reason is simple: even though existing business practices have been automated, the process of automation alone does not correct fundamental design or performance deficiencies. Only by realigning the organization with the changing environment; redesigning the organization, its structures, and its tools; redefining individual roles and responsibilities; and then reengineering processes and procedures, can significant increases in effectiveness, efficiency, and productivity be achieved.

The evaluation of reengineering

Reengineering has been defined, in the past, as using the power of modern information technology to radically redesign administrative business processes in order to achieve dramatic improvements in their performance. Applied in a transformative context, however, reengineering goes far beyond this early definition. It involves reconceptualizing processes and their roles in the achievement of the organization's mission. Reengineering, then, does not merely achieve higher productivity and performance. It actually may alter the very outcomes of the enterprise being reengineered.

Put another way, it is within the realigned, redesigned, and redefined con-

> Only in a transformative context will reengineering yield significant increases in effectiveness, efficiency, and productivity. It is necessary to
>
> ■ realign the organization with its changing environment;
> ■ redesign the organization, its structures, and its tools;
> ■ redefine individual roles and responsibilities; and
> ■ reengineer processes in the transformative context.

text that a critical reexamination of *all* basic assumptions about what is done and how it is done must be made. Processes must be reengineered based upon these new assumptions about service and quality, molded to fit both existing and emerging technological capabilities.

Organization-wide information technology strategy

Reengineering requires an organization-wide information technology strategy, vendors with vision, new levels of systems integration, and new standards of produc-

Reengineering and the Development of an Organization-Wide Information Technology Strategy

■ **Reengineering must involve the reconceptualizing of academic and administrative processes.**

■ **Reengineering can both enhance productivity and alter outcomes.**

■ **This type of reengineering requires an organization-wide strategy.**

■ **New generations of powerful, integrated software products are necessary to serve this strategy.**

supported by robust, fully integrated, commercially developed systems.

Fragmented or incremental information strategies, where institutions purchase particular system modules one at a time, are also increasingly becoming a distinct liability. Many institutions treat each module acquisition as a new competition, selecting the "best" product for different parts of their system architecture. Even if these modules have the best features and functions, they will fail to serve the institution's overwhelming need to achieve complete and full integration of its administrative and academic information systems.

tivity and effectiveness. The complexity and span of the necessary information infrastructure will grow dramatically. In this context, systems developers must draw upon a comprehensive inventory of critical expertise. For most institutions, such an inventory of expertise is too costly to acquire and maintain (it is sure to involve over 100 people). Therefore, "home-grown systems" will not be able to remain competitive in the learning marketplace. They will be an anchor in the altogether negative sense, preventing transformative applications. These "built-it-ourselves" systems will have an increasingly negative impact on the performance of the institutions trying to compete with other institutions and other learning competitors, especially those

Reconceptualizing the information infrastructure

Artificial barriers between academic and administrative systems must be eliminated if an institution is to transform. Academic and administrative functions must be fused into one fully integrated infrastructure. Barriers such as separate academic and administrative networks, organizations, lines of reporting, and systems will work against many institutions striving for system integration and transformation. New generations of powerful, fully integrated software products that are designed with an open systems architecture, independent of database and platform, interoperable, scalable, and designed to support learning facilitation and management will be essential to progress. These new systems will achieve substantial synergy between different technologies: pervasive and ubiquitous networking, client-server architecture, powerful software applications, and smart cards.

The 20th century set of systems that exist today are: Alumni Development, Facilities Management, Financial Aid, Financial Records, Human Resources, Library, and Student Records. Often the acquisition and control of these systems are divided among the administrative units they serve. The acquisition is determined by a committee of concerned individuals through a separate RFP process. The RFP is evaluated in isolation of other systems and the decision of what to buy is also made in isolation.

The right-hand figure outlines the potential ingredients of a comprehensive 21st century system.

Reengineering Academic Processes

One of the first challenges that must be confronted in systematically reengineering academic processes is to determine the desired academic outcomes. Institutions today focus almost exclusively on internally defined indicators of performance. In the 21st century, these must be

A New Generation of Powerful Systems

Academic Information and Collaboration

- Library systems
- Internet/Web access
- Electronic mail
- Digital learning systems
- Customized text/video
- Collaborative work-space tools

Facilities Management

- Facilities design system
- Energy management system
- Preventive maintenance
- Risk management
- Security
- Water management system
- Work order control

Fiscal Management

- Automated security and control
- Financial aid management system
- Integrated fiscal operations
- Integrated planning and budgeting
- Paperless environment
- Point-of-sale payment systems

Enrollment Management

- Alumni records
- Perpetual education records
- Prospecting
- Retention management subsystem
- Student records

Human Resources Development

- Benefits management subsystem
- Forecasting
- Human resource records
- Skills inventory
- Collaboratory profiles

Learning Development

- Course-learning module authoring subsystem
- Examples of "best practices"
- National instructional module repository

Learning Management

- Academic advising
- Curriculum subsystem
- Learning diagnostics
- Learner portfolios
- Testing/grading/mastery certification

Examples of 20th Century Key Performance Indicators

- **Administrative cost per FTE student**
- **Average class rank, incoming freshmen**
- **Average HS GPA, incoming freshmen**
- **Average test scores, incoming freshmen**
- **Campus crime rate**
- **Four-year graduation rate of students**
- **Number of degrees awarded**
- **Number of open access PCs**
- **Number of parking spaces**
- **Number of students in each major**
- **Student/faculty ratio**
- **Tuition dependence**
- **Tuition rate**
- **Tuition revenue**

significantly enhanced to incorporate client and societal key performance indicators (KPIs). The left-hand figure gives some examples of traditional KPIs. The figure on the next page suggests some KPIs that may be appropriate for the 21st century. The list is derived from suggestions from enrollment management professionals in several national workshops on strategic enrollment management.

The nature of the additional KPIs, as suggested by professionals whose responsibility it is to attract quality students to their campuses, suggests a fundamental shift in the criteria that will be used by students to assess a campus. Yet, a word of caution is in order. These expectations will not impact all institutions equally. For example, low-priced institutions will continue to be in high demand by students, but demand does not equal satisfaction. Some institutions will adhere to traditional approaches despite learner needs. Learners, policy makers, and funding providers will continue to press for these fundamental changes in approach.

Reengineered academic processes will be one of the key facilitators of transformation. The blueprint for reengineered academic processes will vary from campus to campus.

Affect what matters most

As we approach the fundamental academic reengineering issues it is useful to examine the research for insight into what matters most in affecting educational outcomes. One of the most useful sources for this purpose is Ernest Pascarella and Patrick Terenzini's 1991 volume of meta-analysis titled *How College Affects Students.*

Consider, for example, some of the conclusions that Pascarella and Terenzini draw after considering the research: "The weight of evidence makes it reasonably clear that in postsecondary education neither large or small classes nor lecture or discussion formats are more effective than the other in fostering the mastery of factual subject matter material." They also observe, "It is probably the case, however, that smaller classes are somewhat more effective than larger ones, when the goals of instruction are motivational, attitudinal, or higher-level cognitive processes."

If we shift the frame of analysis from the "classroom" to different approaches of learning, we also find significant evidence of alternatives that have dramatic effects on learner performance.

More personalized systems of learning

In the 1960s a learning model emerged that argued that virtually all students can achieve mastery of any learning task if each is given sufficient time and receives appropriate instruction. Carroll's (1963) model and the closely related mastery concepts of Bloom (1968) have led to the development of various approaches to individualized instruction. By individualized we mean tailored to the needs of a specific learner, not necessarily a one-on-one personal tutorial. These approaches are exemplified by the following:

Audio-Tutorial Instruction (ATI). ATI involves three components: independent study, small group sessions, and general group sessions. During independent study sessions students work independently on learning tasks in a laboratory equipped with tapes, materials, and visual aids. During small group sessions, students meet periodically in groups of six to ten with an instructor for the purpose of training, discussion, and quizzing. Larger general sessions are designed as a forum for the group as a whole to

engage in activities such as lectures, films, and major examinations. Students using the ATI approach experienced an achievement advantage of eight percentile points over conventional control groups. (The control group tested at the 60th percentile and the ATI group at the 68th percentile.)

Computer-Based Instruction (CBI). CBI involves the interactive use of a computer. Programmed instruction, simulation, drill and practice, and tutorial exercises are frequently implemented in CBI. Students using the CBI approach experienced an achievement advantage of 10 percentile points over conventional control groups. (The control group tested at the 60th percentile and the CBI group at the

Examples of 21st Century Key Performance Indicators

- Ability to communicate one-on-one with faculty
- Access to global information network
- Access to unlimited library collections
- Demonstrated value of program
- Flexible curriculum
- Flexible payment options
- Flexible schedule
- Free text search capability
- Lifelong learning support
- Mastery of subject matter material
- Network access from dorm room/home
- Number of students with PCs
- Personal attention from faculty/mentors
- Personalized learning systems available
- Simulation capability available

70th percentile.) Studies also showed significant positive effects on learner attitude and a reduction in instruction time needed.

Personalized System of Instruction (PSI). PSI is conducted through small, modularized units of instruction. Students use study guides to lead them through the material. The focus is upon mastery of material with immediate feedback given on performance and tests. Students move through the material at their own pace. Tutors, proctors, or monitors are available to help individual students with problems. Occasional lectures and discussions punctuate the PSI to provide motivation. Students using the PSI approach experienced an achievement advantage of 19 percentile points over conventional control groups. (The control group tested at the 60th percentile and the PSI group at the 79th percentile.)

There is further evidence that access to individual learning tools dramatically improves performance. In his radical assessment of the nation's educational system, Lewis J. Perelman cited the finding that access to home learning tools could account for significant differences between low- and high-performance schools. (See figure below.)

An emergent strategy for reengineering core academic processes

As we have seen from Pascarella and Terenzini, class size does not appear to

Learning Tools Contribute to Success

Differentiating Characteristics	Low Performing Schools %	High Performing Schools %
Two parents in home	74.4	83.1
Mother working while child in high school	67.6	69.1
Number of home learning tools, above average	34.6	76.4
Father closely monitors school work	64.7	71.7
Mother closely monitors school work	84.9	84.8
Father expects student to attend college	65.3	76.4
Mother expects student to attend college	67.8	79.4

Source: Perelman. *School's Out*, p. 180. From Chubb and Moe, *Politics, Markets, and America's Schools*, Table 4–5.

matter in the mastery of subject matter material, but probably has an effect upon motivation, attitude, and higher-level cognitive processes. We have also seen that learning tools and more individualized systems of learning create dramatic positive effects upon learner performance, as measured by mastery of subject matter material. This suggests that by shifting the learner to individualized systems for mastery of subject matter material and by shifting faculty resources to focus upon motivation, attitude, and higher-level cognitive processes, significant performance gains could reasonably be expected.

The emergence of multiple, national curricula

Textbooks, accrediting organizations, and professional associations all contribute to the evolution and adoption of national standards in curriculum content and classroom practice. They may not be called national standards, but they emerge as standards just the same. With an evolution of focus on learner performance, as measured by mastery of subject matter material, these standards will become the model for a national curricula. As these national curricula evolve, access by institutions and learners to national curricula will become more open.

At the present time, textbook publishers, accrediting agencies, and professional societies can be conservative forces in

> ## An Emergent Strategy for Reengineering Core Academic Processes Will
>
> - ■ shift the learner to individualized systems for mastery of basic subject matter; and
>
> - ■ shift faculty resources to focus on motivation, attitude, and higher-level cognition processes.

academe. But they can become agents of transformation. Digital publishing-on-demand will provide the opportunity for publishers to dramatically alter academic practice. JIT learning tools will provide the instrument for accrediting and professional organizations to seek new models involving less time in basic learning and preplanned, perpetual learning through life. These tools can enable new, transformative approaches.

Dramatically shortened academic time cycles

Academic time cycles now revolve around the term, course, major, degree, and academic contracts specifying workload, and terms and conditions of employment. The information economy, however, has created an environment where time is of very high value. Clients preparing for success in the information economy do not have the luxury of operating in existing academic timeframes. Traditional time-bounded processes such as application/acceptance/enrollment, freshman/sophomore/junior/senior, academic course objective/course/major/degree, will all be challenged and will eventually be reengineered and decoupled from academic calendars. With this decoupling will come a dramatically more responsive academic enterprise.

Intellectual currency

Intellectual currency will be earned throughout the lifetime by the client learner. It will be available in many forms—not just degrees, certificates, or credentials. Intellectual currency will have common values. These will be much more important than the few denominations (course, minors, majors, degrees, certificates, or credentials) that are in circulation today. Intellectual currency will be international in scope and domain, as portable and fluid as money and more valuable than gold. Intellectual currency will be the new coin of the realm of the Information Age.

Overcoming the Mythical Barriers to Transformation

There are many barriers to transformation. But some imagined barriers are mythical. Successful transformative processes can debunk these myths.

Myth 1: student/faculty ratio = quality

The ratio of students to faculty is a surro-gate measure at best. Student/faculty ratios mask many variations in academic practice. Research shows that when mastery of factual subject matter is the evaluative framework, small classes do not make a difference. We also see that when the goals of instruction are motivational, attitudinal, or higher-level cognitive processes, small groups matter. Therefore, within any given student/faculty ratio a wide range of quality can be achieved depending upon how faculty resources are used.

Myth 2: Education or training

Given the complexity of the Information Age and the need to know both the theory and the application, institutions of higher education at all levels must focus more on both education and training. Using the tools of the Information Age will require more attention to training while individuals appropriately trained will be equipped to excel at their education.

Myth 3: Technology as a capital expense

The Information Age has fused the destinies of learning and technology. Access to information and the ability to manipulate it, evaluate it, and shape it into useful form are from now on dependent on the skills to use technology tools. Therefore, the acquisition and renewal of technology must be integrated into the operating expenses of Information Age learning organizations.

Myth 4: The "faculty" are resistant to change

Many faculty are either leading or enabling the transformation of higher education. They do so by curricula innovation, through network scholarship and research, by engineering highly effective learning applications and modules, and by dedicating themselves to the education of individual students under their guidance. Some faculty are highly resistant to change—but by no means all. Many believe that the resistors are a small, vocal, active subset of the faculty as a whole. The major impediment to faculty embracing new roles and responsibilities is the absence of an effective articulation of these roles and their place in a transformed learning vision for the 21st century.

Myth 5: Teaching = learning

The teaching paradigm as it has been defined (teacher/student/classroom/15 weeks/3 hours per week) has never equaled learning. Learning is an individualized effort and to be most effective, must be customizable to the needs and abilities of the learner. Outcomes must be defined, measured, and acted upon. This does not argue against the teacher but expands the options open to the learner.

Confronting the Real Barriers to Transformation

Beyond the mythical barriers to transformation, there are real barriers to be scaled.

There is no question that higher education is an "industry" in denial. Despite repeated warnings that higher education must show increases in productivity corresponding to those shown in other sectors of the economy in order to continue to warrant support, academe resists. Two-thirds of the states have reduced appropriations for higher education, yet productivity gains are still elusive and initiatives to address concerns meet strong opposition from a higher education culture that maintains a prevailing reactive mentality.

The California State University launched the $4 million project DELTA, Direct Electronic Learning Teaching Alternative. But within a few months, due to strong Faculty Senate opposition, DELTA's meaning was changed to Direct Enhancement of Learning Through Technology Assistance and Alternatives. Why? According to one faculty member, "The most important people in all of this are the faculty. If the faculty do not buy in, it isn't going to work." Another faculty union representative is concerned that technology not be allowed to diminish the quality of instruction or to displace faculty members, concluding, "I don't think there is anything to be gained in approaching this new technology in the way that the Luddites approached machinery so long ago . . ." (*The Chronicle of Higher Education,* October 19, 1994, p. A38).

Meanwhile, the student leaders at 17 campuses put their school newspapers on the World Wide Web (among them the University of Arizona, MIT, and California State Universities at Long Beach and Chico) (*The Chronicle of Higher Education,* November 30, 1994, p. A24). The vast majority of students at Harvey Mudd College now bring personal computers and "a significant amount of educational software" with them while dorm network connections continue to grow at 30 percent per year. Most other engineering schools follow a similar pattern. At another state university, three semi-retired faculty devoted two years to developing a comprehensive digital tutorial to assist the students who historically have struggled through the material they presented. Still another department has rewritten its entire major curriculum sequence to incorporate on-line simulation into each course.

Many other very significant undertakings are emerging nationally. For example, the development of the $100 million Iowa Communications Network, the $30 million Maryland Distance Learning Interactive Video Network, the North Carolina Information Highway, the nine-year-old New York State NYSER-NET, the Utah Electronic Highway for Education, the Wisconsin BadgerNet, and the Education Network of Maine, to name a few (*The Chronicle of Higher Education,* December 14, 1994, p. A21). All of these initiatives have met with similar detractors as in California, but each continues to grow and develop.

One of the problems that plagues the transformation process is a lack of models and successes to point the way. For example, many transformative initiatives are still referred to as "Distance Learning," where technology actually makes distance irrelevant. In looking to the future, higher education still adheres to a provider-driven model where clients conform to strict rules of compliance instead of a client- or learner-driven model where the services are available when needed. These barriers are often maintained by a strong professional infrastructure of contracts, unions, and administrative process. This is further exacerbated by a reluctance to invest in infrastructure, pitting infrastructure investments against labor contracts, and purchasing technology via a funds-available process rather than against a strategic design.

These barriers are real. But they will prove surmountable to the campuses that discover the transformative model that fits their distinct needs.

8

Introducing a Transformative Model to Your Campus

- **Perform Strategic Thinking, Then Strategic Planning**

- **Fuse Technology Push with Learning Vision Pull**

- **Use Current Learners to Develop the Competencies Needed by the Information Age Learner**

- **The Choice Is Clear: Transformation or Stagnation**

*I*n its own way, every campus is poised on the brink of transformation. But existing perspectives have been shaped by recurring cycles of retrenchment, reorganization, and restructuring. These perceptions must be elevated to address transformation. So the question facing every educational leader in America is clear: "How can I introduce a transformative vision to my campus?"

To most educational leaders, the answers are anything but clear. During the years of growth, they became accustomed to incremental advancement dealing with regular, predictable one-year or three- to five-year time horizons and outcomes whose shapes and forms were familiar, just bigger and better. During the years of retrenchment, they have developed the capacity to do more with less, but not to fundamentally rethink the basic metaphors for the educational enterprise. Educational leaders are in-experienced in conceiving growth-oriented learning opportunities for the Information Age. Therefore, we must develop the leadership capacity in higher education to launch and nurture trans-formational processes on American campuses. It is also necessary for a broad cross section of faculty, students, admin-istrators, and other stakeholders to participate in those processes.

Traditional planning processes have several glaring flaws. Until these flaws are corrected, so-called strategic planning will not support transformation. First, traditional planning processes have featured too much "planning" and too little genuine strategic thinking. This order should be reversed—the emphasis should be on authentic strategic thinking. Second, existing planning structures and processes have been crafted for a slower pace of change. The time cycle of academic change must be substantially shortened for the Information Age. Third, academic program planning generally has not been linked to institutional stra-tegic planning. These linkages must be established. Fourth, resource allocations have been imperfectly shaped by true institutional strategies. Resource alloca-tion must be forcefully driven by such strategies. And fifth, planning has been tied to expenditure-based planning cycles

rather than strategic cycles. We have entered a period of fundamental strategic change and opportunity. Institutions should awaken to that reality and allow strategic cycles to drive genuine strategic thinking about cam-pus futures, which can then be reinte-grated into tactical planning for expen-diture-driven plan-ning cycles.

The transforma-tional process on campus should begin with strategic think-ing about the future needs of Informa-tion Age learners, the capacity to meet those needs through network-centered learning, and the potential use of investment in technology to serve learners and reap new sources of revenue. This strategic thinking will generate a learning vision of compelling power. This learning vision will "pull" the campus forward and empower strategic planning. Strategic planning processes should be trans-formative in their intent. They should enable participants to conceive of how existing programs and processes can be redirected toward transformative ends. And how investment in infrastructure,

> ## Why Planning May Not Be Transformative
>
> - **There is too much planning, too little strategic thinking.**
> - **Existing structures and processes are built for a slower pace of change.**
> - **Academic program planning is not linked to institutional strategic planning.**
> - **Resource allocations are not linked to strategies.**
> - **Planning cycles are expenditure-based, rather than strategic.**

new learning initiatives, and allocations of resources can push the campus toward transformation. Finally, educators must

> ### Perform Strategic Thinking, Then Strategic Planning, That
>
> ▪ **navigates through the future;**
>
> ▪ **is reality-based, future-focused; and**
>
> ▪ **does not insulate constituents from economic and political realities.**

use current learners as the test bed for developing the infrastructure, learning support tools, and service orientation that will eventually enable higher education to serve legions of lifelong learners.

Perform Strategic Thinking, Then Strategic Planning

Navigating through the future is never easy. But strategic thinking about the potential of Information Age learning should provide a substantial impetus to consider the opportunities and risks associated with two scenarios for the future: 1) continuing to respond incrementally and reactively, or 2) acting decisively and transformatively to create Information Age universities.

With the future comes risk. The risk of moving in the wrong direction. The risk of investing resources in a direction with a limited future. The risk of competitors gaining strategic advantage and undermining resources. At the heart of risk lies error. When considering transformation there are two types of error with which one must be concerned. The first type can be classified as the mistake. It occurs when an organization heads in the wrong direction or launches an initiative that fails. The second type of error can be classified as the missed opportunity. It occurs when an organization fails to establish a new direction or launch a new initiative and loses strategic advantage. Mature organizations—such as higher education—would rather miss an opportunity than make a mistake. In periods of rapid societal change such as the transition from the Industrial to the Information Age, the missed opportunity can be as lethal as the mistake—if not more so. A formal transformation process seeks to steer the organization into the future and to avoid both types of errors.

The transformation process navigates through the future. It requires mapping the environment and understanding the emerging changes that will shape future conditions. It then requires initiatives that keep the organization on course through a changing environment. In order to be effective, all of the organization's constituents must be aware of the changes in the environment and their impact upon the organization. They must participate in the transformation process. Too often key constituents are insulated from the harsh political and economic realities while expecting their compliance and conformance with strategies for the future. Strategic planning processes are initiated without the preparation of engaging in a strategic thinking process.

Campus leadership must find ways to stimulate discussion, debate, and dialogue on the need for a transformative vision. Existing processes and/or initiatives can be reshaped as agents of transformation. Models of success are critical; they can be either homegrown or identified elsewhere. Many of the necessary support tools are still under conceptualization and development. But this does not weaken the need for immediate action. While true transformation is a ten-year process—or more—it begins with establishment of transformative vision and concrete actions today.

Fuse Technology Push with Learning Vision Pull

To accelerate the process of transformation in higher education, it is necessary to develop the "pull" of a compelling vision of Information Age learning and fuse that pull with the enabling "push" of technology. This provides a powerful new driver for change.

Learning vision pull significantly enhances the power of enabling technology. Rather than operating on a six-month to two-year timeframe, learning vision pull operates on a five- to ten-year time horizon—or more. It enables decision makers to "see beyond the curvature of the earth" and then apply that vision to present decisions. Learning vision pull focuses on the enabling learning infrastructure rather than technology projects. Learning innovation and synergies are its essence, rather than technology

Learning
Vision Pull

Technology
Push

Getting Transformative Results with Learning Vision Pull

Technology Application Push	Learning Vision Pull
Six-month to two-year time horizon	Five- to ten-year time horizon
Technology project mentality	Enabling learning infrastructure
Technology innovation and function	Learning innovation and synergies
Project decision focus	Learning effectiveness focus
Individual systems and applications	Open, integrated systems

innovations and functions. Learning vision pull deals with learning effectiveness rather than individual project-based decisions. Learning vision pull is exercised and deployed by presidents and provosts, and then stimulates individual faculty champions who are then motivated by a more compelling vision. Finally, learning vision pull enables leaders to understand the need for powerful, integrated, open systems and applications that enable network learning, rather than individual systems and applications. These more powerful visions will change the nature of the initiatives undertaken by our campuses.

The role of campus leadership in building shared vision

This is a period of strategic challenge and opportunity for higher education. Yet, most academic leaders and faculty understand neither why higher education is under assault from stakeholders, nor the opportunities associated with serving Information Age learners. Campus leaders must do more than encourage discussions on these topics; they must exercise true leadership in shaping the debate and helping the campus build a new set of shared values regarding learning in the Information Age.

Given the ethos of academe, the development of shared values must be a process of co-creation, consultation, and testing of ideas, if it is to succeed. But rank-and-file faculty and administrators have such a low level of cognition about Information Age potentials that they must be led—and strongly. The most important leaders on campuses over the next decade will be the presidents, provosts, vice presidents for academic affairs, deans, department chairs, and other academic leaders who have the insight and the vision to lead and stimulate a far-reaching campus dialogue on the emerging Information Age university. These leaders will serve as systems architects, teachers, and challengers of the status quo. Campuses with this sort of leadership will flourish.

Deploy transformation-guided strategic planning

Strategic planning that is guided by a transformative vision will enable campuses to confront the opportun-

---

Deploy Transformation-Guided Strategic Planning

- Establish transformative expectations—not revolution.
- Raise everyone's knowledge base.
- Formalize an inclusive decision process.
- Align resources (attention focus) with strategies, tactics, goals, and objectives.
- Redirect existing processes to transformative ends.
- Utilize leverage points for change.
- Communicate models of success.
- Support agents of transformation, convert skeptics.
- Focus on strategic decisions that facilitate transformation.

ities and risks of learning in the Information Age.

Establish transformative expectations—not revolution. Higher education cannot be transformed overnight. Given the magnitude of the likely changes in academic roles, substantial and continuing discussion will be required. Many of the support tools, learningware, and next generation of technology applications enabling genuine transformation have yet to be developed. But by understanding the potentials of transformation, campuses can begin to move forward on all the necessary vectors of change—infrastructure, academic programs, learning initiatives, changes in faculty roles—that will assure their capacity to take advantage of transformative opportunities when they become practical.

Raise everyone's knowledge base regarding the reason for undertaking transformational initiatives. Even if strategic planning is preceded by a substantial effort at strategic thinking, the knowledge base of the campus community must be continually raised. Every campus should convene an ongoing colloquium on the necessities of transformation and the opportunities awaiting the transformed university. The learning requirements of the Information Age and the opportunities for Learning Age universities should be made essential topics of campus discussion. This will re-

quire the raising of consciousness among faculty, administration, students, and other stakeholders. A new sense of shared values will emerge from this discussion.

Formalize an inclusive decision process. The strategic planning process on campus must involve broad segments of the campus community. Such an inclusive process is important in overcoming resistance to change and in crafting strategies that gain support. The strategic planning process must not be seen as owned by any individual sector of the community.

Align resources with strategies, tactics, goals, and objectives. As strategic planning generates strategies, tactics, goals, and objectives, these must drive the allocation of resources. The realignment of campus resources to support transformative initiatives—and the investment of new resources in infrastructure and enabling technologies—will distinguish which campuses will win in the Information Age.

Redirect existing processes to transformative ends. Rather than establishing completely new campus processes, many existing processes can be redirected toward transformative ends. In many cases, a fundamental philosophical redirection toward transformative goals and a 10 or 15 degree adjustment in the direction of current initiatives will propel a campus toward transformation. Existing processes that are candidates for redirection would include: strategic planning, budgeting, facilities planning, academic program planning, strategic enrollment management, and information technology planning. In addition, campuses will need to do a much more professional and creative job of revenue planning, especially in planning for new mechanisms for learners to pay for intellectual property and learning value.

Utilize leverage points for change. In the ongoing life of a campus, there are dozens of leverage points that can be used to foster change. Several prime examples include the design and construction of new facilities, accreditation and academic program review, implementation of new information systems, use of advisory committees for colleges or particular academic programs, and initiation of a continuous quality improvement or process reengineering program. These leverage points can be used to accelerate transformation.

If these leverage points are applied to transformative ends, or if two or three are bundled together, genuine synergy can be achieved. For example, an opportunity to build a new student services building could be combined with new, integrated information systems, the reengineering and reorganization of the enrollment services division, and a change in campus policies to create a transformed, one-stop shopping

approach to student services. This has worked on several campuses. Examples of this type abound.

Communicate models of success. The transformation of any campus is aided by models of success—both internal and external. As the transformation movement grows, the network of participating campuses will share examples of how to win in the Information Age.

Support agents of transformation, convert skeptics. On one level, it is important to "water where the grass is green" and support faculty champions of transformation and new approaches to serving Information Age learners. These champions should win funding for new learner initiatives and projects. On another level, however, it is also necessary to confront skeptics and defenders of the status quo and challenge their implicit assertions that Industrial Age models are acceptable for higher education. This dialogue must become pervasive on campus in the 1990s.

Focus on strategic decisions that facilitate transformation. Strategic plans are fine. But decisions and actions will position institutions to foster transformation. Today's decisions will likely determine whether a campus will be positioned to take advantage of transformation activities five and ten years in the future.

Use Current Learners to Develop the Competencies Needed by the Information Age Learner

Each campus will need to follow its own path toward transformation. Each will need to involve the campus community in different ways in that process. For those daunted by the challenge of serving a new tidal wave of highly demanding Information Age learners, we have a simple message: Begin with your current learners. Use them to develop the competencies and philosophies necessary to successfully serve the Information Age learner. The following vectors of change would be common to most campus settings.

Encourage the growing emphasis on learning, rather than teaching, and widespread innovation in learning

Across the nation, American colleges and universities are refocusing on the importance of learning. Encourage this development on your campus. Fund innovation—not just incremental pedagogical enhancement—but real boundary-busting innovation. Participate in national innovation movements such as the National Learning Infrastructure Initiative; the

Use Current Learners to Develop the Competencies to Serve the Information Age Learner

- Encourage the growing emphasis on learning, rather than teaching, and support innovation in learning.
- Develop and reward transformative leadership.
- Apply network scholarship to undergraduate education—transform the undergraduate experience.
- Search for and disseminate success stories and applications.
- Focus on the development of enabling campus infrastructures.
- Foster experimentation with different roles and combinations of roles on campus for faculty, learners, and administrators.
- Use electronic village pilots to integrate K-12, postsecondary, and perpetual learners.
- Work with current technology companies to envision truly transformative applications.
- Demand open, fully integrated, transformative systems and set expectations.
- Work with stakeholders to establish transformative expectations and provide funding for expanding the learning base.

American Association for Higher Education's initiatives on assessment, CQI, and changing faculty roles; and others.

Develop and reward transformative leadership

We need a new generation of academic leadership that is guided by a transformative vision and skilled in organizational change. Provosts, vice presidents for academic affairs, deans, and department chairs are especially important. The existing initiatives fostered by AAHE—faculty roles and rewards, assessment, CQI, and the use of technology in learning—can all be used to advance transformation. The academic department will be the fulcrum of change in the transforming university.

Apply network scholarship to the undergraduate experience

Network scholarship is primary and fundamental to transformation. Begin immediately to apply this approach to undergraduate instruction. Experiment with different approaches to students using the network to prepare for class—and change the classroom from a place where information is exchanged to a place where knowledge and higher level cognitive skills are developed. Use network scholarship to overcome the tyranny of the academic calendar and physical location. Experiment. Test. Innovate. Begin in earnest today.

Search for and disseminate success stories and applications

Foster the exchange of success stories and best practices—on campus, within disciplines, and across disciplines. Focus not just on award-winning technology applications to existing pedagogical models, but on boundary-busting approaches to learning. Participate in national learning innovation networks.

Focus on the development of enabling campus infrastructures

The information technology infrastructure is elemental to transformation. Invest in information technology and find ways to utilize that investment to reap new revenues and help fund learning innovation.

Foster experimentation with different roles on campus

As a complement to supporting innovation in learning, foster experimentation with different campus roles—for faculty, administrators, and learners. Study and assess the results and share with other campuses.

Use electronic village pilots to integrate K-12 and postsecondary learners

Selected leading campuses are participating in electronic village pilot projects with their surrounding communities. These provide wonderful opportunities to experiment with the full linkage and integration of K-12 and postsecondary learners—and with lifelong learners in the community. These pilots can be used to develop access and navigation skills and protocols and to experiment on a small scale with capabilities that can later be rolled out to larger learner populations of perpetual learners.

Work with technology companies to envision truly transformative applications

Higher education needs to push technology companies to expand the imagination and capability of technology applications available to colleges and universities. Few academic leaders fully comprehend the implications of learning in the Information Age. Many leaders of technology companies have not come to cognition on this issue, either. Educational leaders must raise the consciousness of their peers and technology companies to the demands and opportunities of learning in the Information Age.

Demand fully integrated, open, transformative systems and establish such standards

As part of raising the consciousness of educators and technology companies, we must establish the expectation that the new generation of information technology systems will be fully integrated, open, and transformative.

Work with stakeholders to establish transformative expectations and provide funding for expanding the learning base

The various stakeholders of higher education—funders, accreditors, standard setters, and pundits—must be educated on the potentials of transforming higher education to an Information Age model. They must reduce onerous regulations, change accountability standards, foster experimentation and rapid change, encourage investment in technology, and otherwise transform their policies and practices to enable the transition to an Information Age model.

Institutions cannot be transformed overnight. Nor should they be. Our vision of the future is still ephemeral. But by accepting transformation as a guiding vision and using existing learners to perfect the tools of transformation, academic leaders can position their

American Higher Education

The Choice:

- Accept the risks of transformation to an Information Age model, or
- Be resigned to the certainty of stagnation and decline.

The Challenges:

- Embrace transformation to serve legions of new Information Age learners.
- Prepare all graduates for a lifetime of perpetual scholarship in pursuit of fused work and learning.
- Prepare all graduates for just-in-time learning, network scholarship, and the integrating of timeless and timely knowledge.

campuses to respond to the opportunities of Information Age learning.

The Choice Is Clear: Transformation or Stagnation

So the choice is clear: Accept the risks of pursuing the transformation of higher education to an Information Age model, or the certainty of stagnation and decline as Industrial Age colleges and universities fall farther and farther from favor. This issue should become the focus of rigorous debate on every campus in America.

Just because we are changing a great deal does not mean we are transforming. Nothing short of genuine transformation will enable colleges and universities to address the needs of Information Age learners. Merely making existing delivery mechanisms more efficient through information technology will prove insufficient.

During a period of fundamental change, it is typically more dangerous to stand still than to risk change. Colleges and universities should not delude themselves with the comforting thought that "this too shall pass." After all, even the Industrial Revolution did not alter the basic patterns and cadences of academic life. However, the tools of the Industrial Age did not fundamentally affect knowledge work as will the tools of the Information Age. Academic work in the sciences, the professions, and other applied disci-

plines clearly will be transformed. Even the traditional, contemplative disciplines, the arts, and music will discover that the digitization of text and video will revolutionize both aspects of their core disciplines and their relationships with other disciplines. New, hybrid disciplines may emerge. Digital capabilities are creating new ways of expressing, interpreting, and knowing. Clearly, new does not always mean better. Vigorous debate and exploration of these issues will enliven academe over the next decade.

Individual colleges and universities will miss the opportunity to serve Information Age knowledge workers if they do not transform. But institutions that do not provide at least some transformed options will risk losing competitive advantage in appealing to traditional students as well. Even traditional undergraduates at iconographic liberal arts colleges will want to utilize network scholarship to enrich their undergraduate learning and developmental experiences. Moreover, these students will demand that their experiences prepare them for a lifetime of perpetual scholarship in pursuit of fused work and learning opportunities. Preparing graduates for just-in-time learning and network scholarship, and the integrating of timeless and timely knowledge, is a challenge worthy of American higher education on the brink of the 21st century.

Afterword

Further Readings

Bekhard, Richard, and Wendy Pritchard. *Changing the Essence: The Art of Creating and Leading Fundamental Change in Organizations.* San Francisco: Jossey-Bass, 1992.

Benveniste, Guy. *The Twenty-First Century Organization.* San Francisco: Jossey-Bass, 1994.

Bolter, J. D. *Writing Space: The Computer, Hypertext, and Writing.* Erlbaum Associates, 1991.

Borden, Victor M. H., and Trudy W. Banta. *Using Performance Indicators to Guide Strategic Decision Making.* New Directions for Institutional Research, Volume 82, San Francisco: Jossey-Bass, Summer 1994.

Bridge, William. "The End of the Job," *Fortune.* September 19, 1994, pp.62-74.

Business Week. Special Report. "Rethinking Work," October 17, 1994, pp. 75-102.

Davis, Stan, and Jim Botkin. *The Monster Under the Bed: How Business is Mastering the Opportunity of Knowledge for Profit.* New York: Simon & Schuster, 1994.

Drucker, Peter F. *Post-Capitalist Society.* New York: Harper Collins, 1993.

Drucker, Peter F. "The Age of Social Transformation," *The Atlantic Monthly.* November 1994, pp. 53-80.

Ehrmann, Steven C. "Asking the Right Questions: What Does Research Tell Us About Technology and Higher Learning?" *Change.* March/April 1995, pp. 20-27.

Galbraith, Jay R., Edward E. Lawler III & Associates. *Organizing for the Future: The New Logic for Managing Complex Organizations.* San Francisco: Jossey-Bass, 1993.

Gilbert, Steven W. "Teaching, Learning, & Technology: The Need for Campuswide Planning and Faculty Support Services," *Change*. March/April 1995, pp. 47-52.

Green, Kenneth C., and Steven W. Gilbert. "Great Expectations: Content, Communications, Productivity, and the Role of Information Technology in Higher Education," *Change*. March/April 1995, pp. 8-18.

Guskin, Alan E. "Restructuring the Roles of Faculty," *Change.* September/October 1994, pp. 17-25.

Hamel, Gary, and C. K. Prahalad. *Competing for the Future.* Cambridge: Harvard Business School Press, 1994.

Handy, Charles. *The Age of Paradox.* Cambridge: Harvard Business School Press, 1994.

Handy, Charles. *The Age of Unreason.* Cambridge: Harvard Business School Press, 1989.

Kotter, John P. "Leading Change: Why Transformation Efforts Fail," *Harvard*

Business Review. March-April 1995, pp. 59-67.

Lanham, Richard A. *The Electronic Word: Democracy, Technology and the Arts*. The University of Chicago Press, 1993.

Lynton, Ernest A. *Making the Case for Professional Service*. Amercan Association for Higher Education, 1995.

Marshall, Edward M. *Transforming the Way We Work: The Power of the Collaborative Workplace*. New York: American Management Association, 1995.

Negroponte, Nicholas. *Being Digital*. New York: Alfred A. Knopf, 1995.

Pascarella, Ernest T., and Patrick T. Terenzini. *How College Affects Students*. San Francisco: Jossey-Bass, 1991.

Penrod, James I., and Michael G. Dolence. *Reengineering: A Process for Transforming Higher Education*. CAUSE Professional Paper #9, Boulder, Colorado, 1992.

Penzias, Arno. *Harmony: Business, Technology and Life After Paperwork*. New York: Harper Business, 1995.

Perelman, Lewis J. *School's Out: A Radical New Formula for the Revitalization of America's Educational System*. New York: Avon Books, 1992.

Plater, William W. "Future Work: Faculty Time in the 21st Century," *Change*. May/June, 1995. pp. 22-33.

Quinn, James Brian. *Intelligent Enterprise*. New York: Free Press, 1992.

Rheingold, Howard. *The Virtual Community: Homesteading on the Electronic Frontier*. Addison-Wesley Publishing Company, 1993.

Scott Morton, Michael S. *The Corporation of the 1990s: Information Technology and Organizational Transformation*. New York: Oxford University Press, 1991.

Senge, Peter M. *The Fifth Discipline: The Art & Practice of the Learning Organization*. New York: Doubleday Currency, 1990.

Senge, Peter M., Richard Ross, Bryan Smith, Charlotte Roberts, and Art Kleiner. *The Fifth Discipline Fieldbook: Strategies and Tools for Building a Learning Organization*. New York: Doubleday Currency, 1994.

Toffler, Alvin. *Power Shift*. New York: Bantam Books, 1990.

Twigg, Carol A. *The Need for a National Learning Infrastructure*. Washington: EDUCOM, 1995.

Watkins, Karen E., and Victoria J. Marsick. *Sculpting the Learning Organization: Lessons in the Art and Science of Systemic Change*. San Francisco: Jossey-Bass, 1993.

Yarmolinsky, Adam. "Reinventing Liberal Education," *Planning for Higher Education*. Volume 23, Spring 1995. pp. 71-74.

About the Authors

Michael G. Dolence and Donald M. Norris have helped many organizations develop strategies to meet the enhanced performance challenges of the Information Age. Strategic planning and strategic marketing to achieve realignment with the needs of the Information Age are the centerpieces of their consulting practices. Their clients have included information technology companies serving higher education, other major corporations, colleges and universities, state agencies, and associations and other nonprofit organizations. They have assisted scores of institutions in strategic planning and organizational transformation.

Norris and Dolence have written and spoken extensively on transforming higher education. They have written many books, monographs, and articles on the application of the tools of transformation—key performance indicator-driven strategic planning, reengineering, continuous quality improvement, information resources planning, strategic enrollment management, developing strategic alliance and partnerships, and building inclusive, high-performing organizations from diverse workforces.

Before establishing their consulting firms, both Norris and Dolence gained experience and perspective in a variety of research, administration, and planning capacities in higher education. Norris served at the University of Houston, University of Texas at Austin, University of Michigan, and Virginia Polytechnic Institute and State University. Currently, he is a fellow at the Institute for Educational Transformation at George Mason University. Dolence served California State University–Los Angeles and the Commission on Independent Colleges and Universities for the State of New York. Both have been recognized for their service and contributions by several educational associations.

Donald M. Norris, Ph.D.
President
Strategic Initiatives, Inc.
12209 Jonathon's Glen Way
Herndon, VA 22070
Voice: 703-450-5255
FAX: 703-404-2287
e-mail:<stratinit@aol.com>

Michael G. Dolence
President
Michael G. Dolence & Associates
Post Office Box 922
Claremont, CA 91711-0922
Voice: 909-625-9637
FAX: 909-625-7327
e-mail:<miked@tiger.cuc.claremont.edu>

About the Designers—IDC/AIR

The Information Design Center (IDC), a part of the American Institutes for Research (AIR), conducts, applies, and disseminates research on how to make information products and systems usable.

For more than 15 years, IDC has developed and applied research-based tools for writing and design. We have produced several publications, including *Guidelines for Document Designers*, which has been used by thousands of individuals, companies, and universities.

A management consulting group, IDC specializes in communication strategies, research, and applications. Our research-based approach ensures that we create functional paper and electronic documents that meet the needs of all users. Our services include

- planning/revising, organizing, writing, designing, testing, and managing the production of systems of documents;

- guiding the transition from paper to electronic documents;

- research and testing that includes focus groups, usability testing, expert reviews, and reviews of the literature; and

- publications and workshops on a wide variety of document and information design topics.

American Institutes for Research Information Design Center
Susan Kleimann, Ph.D.
3333 K Street, NW
Washington, DC 20007
Voice: 202-342-5067
FAX: 202-342-5033
e-mail: <skleimann@air-dc.org>

About the Publisher—SCUP

The Society for College and University Planning is the only association focused on the promotion, advancement, and application of effective planning in higher education. SCUP's organizing principle is that planning is essential to improving and maintaining the health, vitality, and quality of higher education.

SCUP has a membership of more than 3,000 individuals, representing each type of post-secondary institution—public and private, two-year and four-year, small and large—as well as college and university systems, governing/coordinating boards, companies, and other related organizations.

SCUP's print publications include the flagship quarterly, *Planning for Higher Education*, and a quarterly newsletter, "SCUP News." SCUP publishes books such as this one. Another of SCUP's publications, *A Guide for New Planners*, has provided many new planners with their first introduction to the field.

SCUP's Planning Pages on the World Wide Web are a growing on-line resource for higher education planners, providing planning-related content as well as links to other on-line higher education resources. SCUP's moderated, twice-a-month electronic newsletter, "SCUP E-mail News," is in its tenth year of transmission.

SCUP's international conference, held each summer, provides essential professional development and networking opportunities for those involved in higher education planning. A number of smaller workshops and conferences are also offered each year in diverse geographic locations. SCUP welcomes inquiries about its resources.

**Society for College
and University Planning**
4251 Plymouth Road, Suite D
Ann Arbor, MI 48105-2785
Voice: 313-998-7832
FAX: 313-998-6532
e-mail: <scup@umich.edu>
WWW: <http://www.umich.edu/~scup/>

About the Sponsor— CyberMark, Inc.

As colleges and universities change to meet the needs of tomorrow's learners, they will find the pathway to transformation filled with challenge and opportunity.

CyberMark is facilitating this transformation. We are creating technology infrastructures that combine the delivery of intellectual property and support services with on-line and off-line payment capabilities. These tools help institutions enhance productivity, generate new sources of revenue, and streamline academic and administrative processes.

CyberMark has joined with industry leaders in the publishing telecommunications, hardware, software, banking, and retail industries to encourage the introduction of new technology and services for higher education. Our new system combines highly secure smart card technology and metering capabilities.

The CyberMark solution can literally free the institution from the limitations of time and place. Activities that now require a trip to an administrative office may be accomplished from home, on-line, and after hours. Intellectual property can be accessed and paid for electronically. Financial transactions become cash-free.

CyberMark can show you how to incorporate technology into your business plan. We'll work with you on creative financing, and help you realize new revenues from your technology investment. The CyberMark solution provides a scalable platform for future expansion-growing and changing with the institution and the marketplace.

CyberMark, Inc.
1050 Thomas Jefferson Street, NW
Washington, D.C. 20007-3871
Voice: 202-298-3300
FAX: 202-298-3308
e-mail: <info@cybermark.com>

Need to Plan?

*Tap the resources of **SCUP**, higher education's premier planning society*

Struggling to plan in turbulent waters? Attend SCUP–32,

Planning in a Rocking Boat: What Will Work?,

Chicago, July 12–16, 1997.

Attend **SCUP**'s annual international Conference and Expo and stay posted through plenary sessions, concurrent sessions, preconference workshops, insider tours of local campuses, and networking with over 1,000 professionals. This year's sessions include:

- Community colleges evaluate the AACC's effectiveness indicators
- Estimating the effects of the baby boomer echo on enrollments
- Using facilities benchmarking instead of space standards
- Using real estate in strategic alliances with technology companies

Need a common language and vision for change in the information age?

Want expert hands-on help and collegial support?

Try **SCUP**'s "Transformation" book and workshop. Hundreds of institutions have made *Transforming Higher Education—A Vision for Learning in the 21st Century* required reading for planning retreats.

Join **SCUP**'s "Transformation" Workshop and Collaboratory; May 2–4, 1997, Atlanta; August 8–10, 1997, Newport Beach, California.

Want the scoop on academic planning?

Read *Doing Academic Planning—Effective Tools for Decision Making* (edited by Brian P. Nedwek, 1996) with its chapters on:

- Information technology
- Performance indicators
- Articulation agreements
- Enrollment projections
- Scanning
- Program review
- Quality
- Co-curriculum
- Human resources

Contact SCUP to stay on top of planning

Society for College and University Planning

4251 Plymouth Road
Ann Arbor, MI 48105-2785
Voice 313.998.7832
Fax 313.998.6532
Web http://www.scup.org
Email scup@umich.edu

Transforming Higher Education
A Vision for Learning in the 21st Century

Michael G. Dolence and Donald M. Norris

Mail or fax this order form to the:
Society for College and University Planning
PO Box 7350
Ann Arbor, MI 48107-7350 USA
Fax (313) 998-6532

Transforming Higher Education went into its second printing within three months of publication, largely due to institutions of higher education ordering quantities of additional books for wider distribution, to facilitate planning efforts—within departments and committees or institutionwide. If your institution is interested in larger quantities (100 or more), please call about quantity discounts and/or the possibility of campuswide site licensing for print-on-demand.

ORDER FORM

PRICES

	QUANTITY	AMOUNT
Single Copies		
Member price $25 US *Includes shipping and handling within the USA*		
Nonmember price $40 US *Includes shipping and handling within the USA*		
10–24 copies (price per book)		
Member price $21 US *Includes shipping and handling within the USA*		
Nonmember price $34 US *Includes shipping and handling within the USA*		
25 or more copies (price per book)		
Member price $20 US *Includes shipping and handling within the USA*		
Nonmember price $32 US *Includes shipping and handling within the USA*		

SHIPPING AND HANDLING COSTS

Within the **USA**, s/h **UPS ground** cost is included in the price of each book
Within **Canada**, add $2 US per book; within Mexico, add $5 per book
Outside North America, add $7 US per book
Within USA for **expedited 2nd-day** add $6 for 1st book and $1 each add'l bk
Within USA for **overnight** add $15 for 1st book and $2 each up to 4 bks max

Call (313) 998-6967 or email <terry@scup.ra.itd.umich.edu> to inquire about expediting larger shipments.

ORDER TOTAL _____

PAYMENT *Payment must be by check, institutional purchase order, or credit card. Resellers: SCUP does not allow the return of unsold books. Credit cards: SCUP only accepts MasterCard, Visa and American Express.*

❑ Check payable in US funds to "SCUP"   ❑ Institutional Purchase Order Number _____

❑ MasterCard   ❑ Visa   or   ❑ American Express   Card Number _____

Name on card _____

Expiration Date _____   Signature _____

SHIP TO

Name _____

Title _____

Organization _____

Address *(no post office box)* _____

City _____   State/Province _____

Zip/Postal Code _____   Country _____

Telephone _____   Fax _____   Email _____

Allow 2–3 weeks for delivery (more outside North America) unless choosing an expedited shipping option.